My Father is the Gardener

COLIN URQUHART

My Father is the Gardener

HODDER AND STOUGHTON
LONDON SYDNEY AUCKLAND TORONTO

To our Lord Jesus Christ,
through whose love we are
made branches of the True
Vine

Introduction

In the life of the Church today, an important spiritual renewal is taking place. This is the work of God the Holy Spirit, and several books have been written in recent years testifying to the ways in which God has begun to transform real situations.

All the characters in this book are fictitious and so is the situation in which they are placed. Their problems and dilemmas, however, are true to life and so this book is about the problems and dilemmas that real people encounter as they face the implications of God's renewing work in their personal lives and in the life of His Church. The fictitious characters and situations have been created so that we can examine their inner feelings and motives in a way that would not be possible in writing about living personalities.

I want to make it perfectly clear that none of the people portrayed in this book is based upon any living person known to me.

My thanks to all who have helped with the preparation of this book, especially to Jane Collins, who has done much to prepare the final text; to Sue, who has spent many hours typing, and to the Sisters of the Holy Ghost, Clapham Park, amongst whom I 'retreated' from a busy pastoral ministry to do most of the writing.

Words cannot convey my gratitude to my wife, Caroline, my children, Claire, Clive and Andrea, the members of the household at St. Hugh's, and to Vivienne and David, who have helped and encouraged me throughout this task.

1

THAT WEEK WAS worse than usual. Tom nearly ran himself into the ground, rushing around to meet appointments, making decisions and working until late at night on reports. He was looking forward to the week-end when he could be himself again, and relax. Yet Saturday arrived, and with it the discovery that he despised the person he had become.

'Thirty-five years old, and what have I achieved? A wife who seems to be growing away from me. A son and daughter I hardly know. A job which always seems to get the better of me. What exactly am I fighting for? I'm nearly frantic with things to do, and yet I never feel I've achieved anything. What is the point?'

He drank and smoked far too much that night and upset Ann by making straight for bed and falling asleep when she desperately wanted to ask him what was wrong. He never heard her sobs.

Sunday came, and routine took them to church. Tom was a Christian, or at least, he'd always thought of himself as one. Every Sunday the third pew from the front on the left-hand side of St. Gabriel's Parish Church could be sure of its usual occupants: Tom, Angela aged seven, Tony aged four, and Ann aged thirty-four, always in that order, reading from aisle to wall. The weekly outing to St. Gabriel's added solidity to their lives and a small measure of comfort to the rector!

'Thank you so much for coming,' was the usual remark as Tom shook his hand after the service. 'So nice to see you all.'

Tom's bitterness had been rising throughout the day and now turned to anger. 'What does the rector know about anything? He lives in a dream world made of words like "hope" and "peace". I have to work hard to achieve anything.'

Ann was worried. She had watched Tom's growing indifference to herself and the children. Sadness seemed to enfold him like a blanket, and fond though she was of him, she felt incapable of piercing it.

'What's the matter, Tom?'

'Nothing,' would be the brusque retort, the question arousing resentment. 'Why does she have to interfere?' he would think. 'How do I know what the matter is? How can I tell her that I am alone, desperately alone, and unhappy? I love her and I know that she loves me; but it's not enough.'

Now that Ann had gone to bed early, he felt even more alone. She was exhausted by the atmosphere of tension that had pervaded the house all day, causing the children to erupt in petty squabbles at five-minute intervals. The house was silent, and Tom could no longer ignore the question that was tormenting him.

'What am I to believe? Who am I to believe?' The words were spoken to a void. He didn't expect an answer.

'Turn to the Word of God for understanding.'

Tom looked round the room. No one was there; yet he had heard a voice—or had he? Perhaps it was not a voice, but from somewhere within him the words had been clear.

10

'Turn to the Word of God for understanding.'

Could that really be the answer to his problems?

Inwardly, Tom groaned at the prospect. The Bible had never been anything more than historic literature to him, neither had the countless sermons he had heard ever succeeded in bringing it to life. He was feeling low enough already; surely the irrelevance of words written so long ago would only add to his hopelessness?

Still the words persisted: 'Turn to the Word of God for understanding.'

Slowly, Tom eased himself out of the chair. He had always prided himself on the rationality of his behaviour, and he felt cross that he was giving in to this impulse to walk across the room and take the Bible from the bookcase. If the decision was his, that would be different; it was this inner compulsion that irritated him.

He returned to his chair, Bible in hand.

'Now what?' he thought.

'John's Gospel, chapter 15,' came the reply.

'I must be going mad,' he thought. His knowledge of the Scriptures had never been great, but he knew where to find John's Gospel.

As he flicked over the pages of the New Testament, he was comforted by the thought that Ann would be asleep and would never know of his evening of silent voices and strange compulsions.

He began to read: 'I am the true Vine, and my Father is the Vinedresser.'

At that point he was prepared to stop, go to bed, and make an appointment with Dr. Chapman first thing in the morning.

'Bit of nervous tension, my boy.' He could imagine the scene and the fatherly voice. 'Take a holiday with that delightful wife of yours. Do you good. Do you good.'

11

He read the words again: 'I am the true Vine and my Father is the Vinedresser.' Meaningless; he had known it would all be meaningless.

'Read on.' Again the authority of this inner voice compelled his obedience.

'Every branch of mine that bears no fruit, he takes away, and every branch that does bear fruit he prunes, that it may bear more fruit.'

'What fruit has there been in my life? I'm a hopeless failure. Thirty-five years on this earth and what have I done or achieved? Nothing!'

The words before him became a blur through the tears which began to fall on to the open Bible, creasing the india-paper pages. He slammed the book shut and sat with his face buried in his hands.

The doorbell rang.

Tom started and made a great effort to control himself. As he went to the front door, he wiped his face on his handkerchief, trying to hide every trace of the tears.

'Who's there?' he asked, not too loudly.

'Just a friend,' replied a reassuring voice. 'I was passing and I thought I would drop in.'

Any further conversation might disturb the sleepers, so Tom opened the door and was surprised to find a work-colleague whose face was familiar, but ...

'Oh, it's Mr. Mitchell, isn't it? What can I do for you?'

'Do you mind if I come in?' the visitor asked.

'Oh no, of course not,' answered Tom. 'I'm sorry, I wasn't expecting anyone so late.'

'Quite so. My name is Alan, by the way.' As he stepped into the light of the hallway, Tom saw that his unexpected guest wore a comfortable tweed jacket and seemed quite at ease.

'You would think it was quite normal to barge in on a comparative stranger so late at night,' thought Tom as he closed the front door.

'Come in and sit down,' he suggested. 'How did you know where I lived?' Tom was still rather puzzled by the man: he could visualise his face behind a desk at work, but knew nothing about him.

'I gave someone a lift here once, and have thought of coming in several times,' explained Alan. 'How are things with you, anyway?'

'Much the same as usual,' mumbled Tom, side-stepping the question. But Alan refused to be put off.

'No, really, Tom. People at the office have noticed that you seem to be under considerable strain.'

'Oh, we all have our ups and downs. It's nothing very important.'

'I don't want to pry, Tom, but if you are as unhappy as you appear, then it is important. Is that the Bible you're reading?'

Tom almost blushed as he looked down at the coffee table between them. He felt as though he had been caught cooking with his wife's apron on. 'Well, not really . . .' Alan, however, seemed prepared to take the subject seriously.

'Is it any help? Which passage were you reading?—we can look at it together.'

Tom reached for the Bible and turned to the tear-stained page. As he tried to straighten the crinkles, his fingers ran over the words 'Peace I leave with you . . . Let not your hearts be troubled.' The meaning struck home and he sighed. This was exactly what he needed: peace.

'What an amazing thing for Jesus to say on the night of His arrest!' Alan had followed his thoughts. 'It was a very tense evening, with everyone sure that something ghastly was about to happen, but not knowing quite what.'

'Like I feel tonight,' ventured Tom.

'Not quite the same though,' countered Alan. 'You see, they had seen what life with Jesus could mean: love, power, healing, miracles. They were filled with a great hope that was centred around Him. You, I would say, have no such hope. You haven't seen Jesus, nor do you have any clear vision of the sort of life that He intends for you. That much is obvious, or you wouldn't be so despondent now. As it is, it all looks pretty hopeless.'

Tom could not deny the truth of that. 'Where do I find this hope?' he asked slightly cynically.

'It comes through realising that God wants to give you a glorious life that you can't have without Him.'

'You disappoint me,' answered Tom. 'Can't you see it's *now* that I feel desperate? Hope of eternal glory doesn't help me at all.' Bitterness had begun to seep into his voice.

'You mistake my meaning,' said Alan calmly. 'I'm not talking about life after death; I refer to what God is wanting to do for you now. Have a look at chapter 15.'

Tom stared down at the page again. 'I am the true Vine, and my Father is the Vinedresser.' He sighed. 'I'm sorry,' he said, 'but I find no hope in these words. You'll have to explain.'

'O.K. Tom. Picture a vine in your mind—roots, stem, branches and fruit. Each is an integral part of the whole and necessary for the vine to be complete. Jesus says He is the Vine. So He is all the various parts; He is the whole thing.'

'What's that got to do with me?' said Tom peevishly. Half of him thought that this extremely good-natured friend could help him, and longed to find out how, and the other half was annoyed at this crackpot who had interrupted him wallowing in his misery.

14

'Simply that Jesus tells the disciples that they are the branches. That would mean that in some sense they must be parts of Him.'

'But where do I fit in?' insisted Tom. Alan looked at him.

'Tom, are you prepared to listen and wait until I get to that point?'

Tom felt the gentle rebuke justified and tried to look more at ease. The faintest suspicion of a smile appeared in Alan's eyes.

'Obviously, Jesus was talking about Himself in a new way. Remember, He was about to be crucified. He knew that was not to be the end: He was to be raised, He would ascend and He would reign in glory with His Father for evermore.'

'He sounds like a walking Apostles' Creed,' thought Tom, unable to understand why he should have such a critical attitude towards all that his guest was saying. The man was right; he needed to listen and not prejudge.

The visitor went on, 'The crucifixion was not to be the end of God in human flesh. Jesus was to live forever—a living eternal Vine. His disciples were to be living branches of this Vine. The Son of God was no longer to live in a single human body, but in several branches, who together would form the living Vine in the world.'

'You're going to have to explain that further,' said Tom.

'Well, you see, Jesus had to find some way of describing Himself in relation to the disciples now that the time had come for Him to return to His heavenly Father.'

The visitor paused. Tom said nothing.

'The Father is the Vinedresser or Gardener; He planted the Vine. The Father sent His Son into the world and asked of Him the ultimate act of love and obedience in giving His life for sinners. The Father desired that the Vine of

15

Jesus should continue in the world after the crucifixion. And it is the Father who cares for the Vine and all the branches that have been incorporated into it.'

Again Alan paused as if to give Tom adequate time to absorb what he had said. The silence was broken only by the faint creaking of a bed upstairs, as one of the children turned over in sleep.

'Tom, you can understand this Vine in at least two ways. First in a mystical sense; Jesus is present in the world to-day, and all who are His disciples are part of this Vine. Secondly on a local basis; the Father plants a body of be-lievers in a particular locality to be a real expression of His Son, a group of people filled with the life, the love and the power of Jesus. Both meanings are essential if we want to grasp fully what He is saying.'

Tom was still wondering how all this was going to relate to his particular problems, but he let the visitor continue.

'God didn't want to remain an abstract idea to His people. He desired to draw them all into a living, personal relationship with Himself. This could only be done through Jesus.' Suddenly, Tom was alert.

'Abstract idea?' Yes, that was all God had ever been to him. 'Personal relationship?' Could it be possible? That seemed only for the great saints of history, not for ordinary Tom Billings. Why should God want any kind of personal relationship with Him?

'I'm sorry,' said Tom. 'I missed that last sentence.'

'I was quoting some words of Jesus: "No one comes to the Father, but by me".'

'Because He forgives our sins, you mean?' suggested Tom, glad that he could contribute what limited know-ledge he had.

'Partly,' the other replied. 'You see, Jesus lived in con-tinual communion with the Father and it was through the

16

cross that He made it possible for all men to live in such fellowship and communion with Him. To be in fellowship with God involves being members of the Body of Christ, branches of the true Vine.'

'How can being a member of St. Gabriel's bring me into fellowship with God? Why, only this morning, the service seemed to last an eternity because I felt so separated from Him. In fact, I spent most of the service wondering if He existed at all!'

'I can understand your problem,' said Alan calmly in response to Tom's outburst. 'I'm not sure that the Lord of heaven and earth regards St. Gabriel's as a prime exhibit of what His Church is intended to be!'

'Well, it's the only church I have,' said Tom defensively. 'Why don't you go and tell all this to the rector?'

'Perhaps I wouldn't be too welcome at the moment.'

'What do you mean? Christopher Dean is a charming man who lives and lets live.'

'But is he asking the right questions?' Alan replied.

'Why have you come here? Am I asking the right questions?'

'Yes, you are beginning to do that. You have come to the end of your own resources and recognised the futility of your life without God. Unless that had happened you would never have listened to what I had to say.'

'Oh.' Tom was silenced.

'You have been searching for God and you have not found Him at St. Gabriel's. You desire some meaning and purpose in your life, but your local church does not appear to have helped you in that sphere. I would not need to be here if the Reverend Dean had helped you to understand more of who Jesus is.'

'Was, you mean!'

'No, Tom, is. Jesus is living today.' There was silence.

17

'I need a cup of coffee,' said Tom. 'Will you have one with me?'

'No, thank you,' Alan replied with a smile.

Tom moved swiftly from the lounge to the kitchen. He needed to take stock of the situation. There, in his house, sat a man he hardly knew, who seemed more able to analyse the situation than Tom himself.

What a pity the brandy bottle was in the other room! He would have liked to supplement the spoonful of instant coffee, but was none too sure whether his visitor would approve. That in itself was strange, as Tom had always prided himself on his independence and refusal to be conditioned by the attitudes and opinions of others. Perhaps that was the difference between this evening's conversation and any other he could remember having. There seemed to be a quiet confidence and authority about this man. He not only believed what he said, but expected Tom to believe it too. That accounted for Tom's rather irrational aversion to listening to the man. He resented the quiet authority that radiated from him.

When he returned to the room Alan was sitting quietly, turning over the pages of Tom's Bible.

'I think we'd better go back to the beginning of John,' he said, when Tom had sat down and felt the benefit of the first scalding sip of his drink. 'The writer refers to Jesus as the Word of God. "In the beginning was the Word, and the Word was with God, and the Word was God." '

He handed the Bible over to Tom so that he could read the words for himself.

'When God spoke, Jesus happened.'

Tom looked puzzled.

'When you speak, your words express what is going on in your mind. They are an expression of your thoughts.'

'Yes, I see that,' said Tom.

18

'Jesus is the Word of God; He expresses in spoken form what is in the mind of God. You could say that He is the verbal expression of the Father. For example, God decides that He wishes to create; He does this through speaking His Word, through Jesus. "All things were made through Him, and without Him was not anything made that was made." That shows us the power of God's Word. He speaks and creation comes into being.'

Tom wouldn't have described himself as one of the brightest men ever to have lived; neither was he a fool. He had been blessed with enough intellect to enable him to establish himself successfully in business. Yet for years he had been perplexed by these opening words of John's Gospel. Now this stranger in a few sentences had explained what he had puzzled over all his life. Tom was eager to hear more.

'This Word, Jesus, became flesh,' the visitor continued. 'Look at verse fourteen. "And the Word became flesh, and dwelt among us, full of grace and truth." When that happened Jesus was no longer only the verbal expression of the Father; He was now also the physical expression of God. So John could go on to say, "We have beheld His glory, glory as of the only Son from the Father." Later Jesus Himself said, "He who has seen me, has seen the Father." Tom, have you ever considered the cost to God of becoming flesh in Jesus?'

'The great God becoming a baby in a stable-manger, you mean?'

'Not just the fact of that, but what it cost God to do that.'

'I don't see what you mean,' replied Tom.

'God is holy and just and perfect,' Alan began, his eyes sparkling. 'He came to dwell among the unholy, the unjust and the imperfect. His motive was a very simple one: love.

He desired to lead His people out of their unholiness, their injustice and imperfection. Incarnation and crucifixion was the only way to achieve that: God Himself living in creation and giving His life for it. And the result? A new creation! New men filled with the Spirit of God, being drawn into one body, the Vine, Jesus.'

'Where is this new creation?' asked Tom. 'I don't see it.'

'That's the problem, Tom; only a few do see it. The life of the Vine should contrast greatly with the life of the old order of creation. That Vine needs to manifest the love of God, His holiness and justice and even His perfection in a world that remains largely hardened against the purposes of God.'

Tom was getting used to this man's strange terminology, but that was a bit much. 'It sounds impossible to me,' he said. 'Perhaps a few very saintly people might achieve something of that kind of life; you could not expect it of many.'

'It is true that each branch has to be grafted in individually,' admitted Alan thoughtfully.

'When can a person be grafted into this Vine?' asked Tom. Something like hope was stirring deep within him.

'Grafting is a delicate business, and God wants every graft to "take". He is content to wait until the individual is ready to be grafted into Jesus. Potentially, that is the place for all men, for Christ died to make it possible for everybody to be incorporated into Him.'

Alan paused, as if expecting some response from Tom. He remained silent, torn by the conflict within him. This stranger seemed to be speaking of some kind of Utopia and yet he spoke of it in such real terms.

'The Father knows the heart of every one of His people,' Alan continued. 'He will not graft into the Vine those who do not desire to belong to Him.'

To Tom, the room seemed to be getting warmer. He felt like going over to the window, throwing it open and breathing in some cool night air. Alan's voice went on.

'The Father desires to place us individually in His Son that we may live in Him, to be a part of His life in the world, to be fruitful branches.'

'Could St. Gabriel's really be part of this Vine?' Tom wondered.

'Never mind St. Gabriel's,' said the visitor. 'What about Tom Billings?'

Tom felt under pressure. His individualistic instincts came to the fore once again. 'You are saying that I can freely choose to become part of the Vine,' he said.

'You are free to place your life in the Gardener's hands that He may graft you into His Son.'

'Then leave me to be free to choose. Don't pressurise me.'

'Tom, I would never dream of doing such a thing. I simply want to point out to you that you have to make a decision for yourself. That's all.'

Tom felt foolish. He knew that it was only the conflict within him that made him react in this way.

'You see, Tom, to be part of the Vine means to have a vital, living relationship with Jesus Himself. You can hardly live in Him without knowing him!'

It was some time before Tom realised that the visitor had lapsed into a long silence. He looked up from the pages of the Bible on his knee, half expecting to see the man gone. No; he sat quietly looking at Tom with great affection.

'Have I allowed the Father to take hold of my life and graft me into Jesus?' Tom reflected.

'Precisely,' the visitor replied.

'Obviously, the answer is "No", or I wouldn't be in this mess tonight.'

'Quite so. You don't know whether you are a branch of the true Vine.'

'I suppose that's it. All these years of going to church and I never knew that the Father wanted to place me in His Son.'

'Sad, isn't it?' said Alan.

'Come on, then! How can I let Him do it?'

'All in good time. It's getting rather late. I think I'd better be on my way.'

'Oh no, you don't.' Tom jumped to his feet to restrain his visitor physically from leaving. 'I want to know how, and I want to know tonight.'

'Are you really prepared to make such a far-reaching decision, Tom? Don't you think it better that you discover more of what life in the Vine is like first?'

'That is the place where I need to be. Somehow, I must get there.'

'Only the Father can place you in the Vine, Tom. That is His prerogative as the Gardener. It's no good striving to attain that position. You can't achieve it by any self-effort or good works.'

The visitor stood up. The two men faced each other. Alan placed a hand on Tom's shoulder.

'I've shown you the way for your personal dilemma to end, Tom. There will be further opportunities for us to talk. I haven't been sent here tonight to leave you in the mess in which I found you. Good night, my friend. God bless you.'

The man quietly left the room and Tom heard the catch of the front door as he let himself out of the house. He slumped back into his chair.

'God, oh God, take hold of my life and place me in Jesus—please.'

2

'YOU CAME TO bed very late last night.' Ann was busy trying to make coffee, toast and porridge all at once, and threw the remark towards Tom as he entered the kitchen. He grunted his assent and sat down.

'Tony, don't do that!' His manner was more abrupt than he had intended, but the command had the desired effect and the young boy stopped banging his spoon on his cereal bowl. The intonation of Tom's voice made Ann look round. Even though he had buried himself in the morning paper, he could not hide the worn, haggard expression on his face; the bags under his eyes seemed to stand out in sharp relief.

'Are you feeling all right, Tom?' Ann sounded genuinely concerned.

'Did you say something?' It was only a defensive question, to give him time to think. He had never been very good at hiding things from Ann. How could he begin to explain the events of the previous evening? He felt so confused about them himself.

'I asked you if you were feeling all right,' repeated Ann. 'You look awful.'

'That's right; build up my confidence,' said Tom, trying to put on an air of good humour.

'I'm being serious,' retorted Ann. 'You look as if you should go straight back to bed.'

'I'm fine. Just a little tired, that's all.'

'Well, why come to bed so late?'

'I was doing some serious thinking.'

Ann was feeling uneasy. Tom's recent moods had opened her mind to all kinds of terrible possibilities. She tried to sound casual. 'And what great thoughts was Tom Billings having in the middle of the night?'

'How much I love you.'

'Tom!'

'What?'

'Don't fool around. I'm being serious.'

'So am I.'

'Mummy, the toast is burning.' Angela's voice broke the tension of the moment. Ann was almost in tears.

'There's nothing to worry about,' said Tom as he stood up. 'I must be going.'

'You haven't had any breakfast,' Ann argued.

'I'm late now. I have to drive north—remember? That new contract. Where's my brief-case? I'll phone to let you know if I have to stay overnight.' He started for the door.

'Tom!'

'What is it?'

Ann wanted to plead with him to stay and explain, but knew it would only make the situation worse. 'You haven't said good-bye to the children.'

He went round the table and kissed Angela, then Tony, on the cheek. He stood looking at Ann.

'Everything is fine. Really.' He kissed her with greater enthusiasm than he felt, picked up his brief-case and went out to the car. Ann felt very alone, and quickly busied herself with the breakfast, trying not to think.

It was pouring with rain. Everything looked grey and

24

soaking wet. 'It fits my mood,' thought Tom. 'Why did I upset Ann so easily when it was the last thing I wanted?' The deep sadness of the previous day began to seep back into his mind. It was as though the hope his visitor had brought in the evening had only made this morning worse by contrast.

Once behind the wheel Tom found that the driving occupied him and calmed his mind—this was much better than having your head full of vines! By the time he had reached the outskirts of the town he was feeling more kindly disposed towards life and when he saw a young hitch-hiker in a layby, his foot touched the brake even before he had given the lad the quick summing-up glance to which he usually subjected potential occupants of his car.

But it was all right: this was a typical student, rather threadbare but clean, with a fringe that he flicked out of his eyes as he leant through the window to ascertain that Tom was going in the right direction. As he climbed in, his only luggage turned out to be a paper carrier bag, and right on top was a well-worn black book with gold lettering on the front—Holy Bible.

Tom felt rather as he did on seeing a bank statement on the doormat in the morning—what was in store for him now? He crunched the gear as he moved back into the stream of traffic, preparing himself to begin the usual hitch-hiker conversation—but his passenger had seen his reaction to the Bible.

'I carry it with me everywhere,' he explained. 'You never know when you may have a spare minute. Do you ever read it yourself, sir?'

Tom didn't know whether he felt trapped or comforted: the lad obviously had conviction, but also some respect for Tom's feelings, which was most welcome. Still, Tom was very surprised to hear himself giving an account of the previous evening. It meant he had to swallow his pride, and this was quite painful, but as he progressed his passenger became more and more excited. When he mentioned his prayer that God would take over, the reaction was an overpowering 'Praise the Lord!' Yet the young man, whom Tom now knew to be called Martin, remained sensitive to the situation.

'How do you feel this morning?' he asked.

'Empty, somehow.' Tom thought a little more. 'Rather let down, on the whole. I gave my life to a living Christ who loved me, or so I thought, and yet so far I have seen very little of either His life or His love.' Suddenly he came up with a start. 'Until you came along, that is. But I looked so ill this morning that my wife wanted to pack me off to bed again, and everything went a bit wrong.'

'Hm. It sounds as though it would be a good idea to pull into this service area,' said Martin unexpectedly.

'Why?' asked Tom. 'I have plenty of petrol and it's too early for coffee.'

'If you believe I can help you at all, Tom, please do as I say. You have a telephone call to make.'

'A telephone call?' Tom was prepared to accept that Martin understood his needs in relation to God, but surely he was overstepping the mark here. 'Who to?'

'To your wife.'

'Ann—why?'

'Please, Tom! You will miss the turning.'

Tom indicated that he was leaving the motorway and slipped up the approach road to the service area. He parked the car and then turned to face Martin.

'Now what is all this about?' he demanded.

'You need revelation from God, Tom, and I believe I am here to give it to you. However, you will find it very much

26

easier to hear what God is wanting to say to you if your relationships are right and good. You will be one step nearer the peace you want if you phone your wife and ask her to forgive you.'

Tom was annoyed. 'Ask her to forgive me! What for?'

'Don't you think you might have upset her this morning?'

'I didn't mean to. Anyway, it was only a little disagreement. She must be used to them by now.'

'That sounds far from ideal,' said Martin. 'Surely you should be able to sort these things out between you. I believe it is time you took the first step towards changing the situation.'

'It isn't all my fault, you know. Why, she ...'

He was cut short. 'You are wasting time, Tom, and you will find a much more willing response in your wife if you stop trying to apportion blame, and simply confess your part in the breakdown of communication.'

This seemed to make sense to Tom, but it would be difficult. No, it was more than sense—there was something truly good about the idea. He hurried to a phone box and dialled his home number.

'Hello, Ann. It's me.'

'Tom!' She sounded pleased; then concerned again. 'Are you all right?'

'Yes, I'm fine.'

'What's the matter, then? It's unusual for you to phone.'

Tom paused. Now it came to the point, he wasn't sure what to say.

'Are you there Tom?' Ann sounded more anxious.

'Yes, yes, I'm here. I ... I just want to say sorry.'

It was Ann's turn to be silent.

'I'm sorry that I upset you this morning. I didn't mean

to. In fact, I've been like a bear with a sore head recently. There's been a lot on my mind.' The pips sounded and Tom realised that he had no more change.

'I'll tell you more when I get home. Good-bye, darling.'

'Good-bye Tom. Thanks for phoning. Drive carefully.'

Tom walked slowly back to the car. Martin did not even look at him as he settled himself in the driving-seat. 'Well, that was rather inconclusive,' said Tom. 'I should have made sure I had more change.' He felt sad, rather than angry. Nothing seemed to go quite right at present.

'Not quite so inconclusive as you think,' the other said encouragingly. 'You have made your wife feel a great deal happier and you have given her some hope.'

'Hope?' Tom was surprised that anybody could gain any hope from such a brief telephone conversation.

'Yes. Hope that when you return home this evening you really will tell her more of what is going on inside you. Ann loves you and she needs to share in your problems.'

They were once again travelling northwards at a steady seventy miles an hour. 'You'd better tell me more about your God,' suggested Tom. His passenger seemed delighted at the suggestion.

Ann replaced the receiver and stood thoughtfully by the telephone. 'Tom, please talk to me tonight, please! I want to know what is going on inside you.'

Her eyes became moist and she reached for a tissue. She had wiped away so many tears in these past weeks, silent tears that Tom wasn't even aware of. Many times she had asked herself the same question that had been burning inside him: 'What is the use of it all?' Was she condemned to a life of daily household routine, continually clearing up after the children, and only a withdrawn uncommunicative husband to spend the evenings with? There seemed to be no zest for living as there had been when they were first married, only a steady accumulation of possessions. And it seemed that the more they possessed, the more they had lost.

She looked around at the tastefully furnished room. A hovel would be better if only there was happiness. And yet she was not unhappy. She loved Tom; she loved the children, despite their selfish ways; she had good health and, until recently, she had felt secure. That was the real problem. She no longer felt secure—about Tom, about the value of possessions, about anything. The thought sent a cold shiver down her spine.

She reached for the telephone. 'I'll ring Ruth,' she thought. 'She's always good fun.' There was no reply. It was going to be a long day.

'God is love,' the student said simply. 'This love of His is different from anything that we usually mean by that word. It is a generous love, a steadfast, sure love that never changes. It isn't fickle like human love, dependent upon emotions and feelings. His love is dependable and strong and will never fail those who are embraced by it.'

'That sounds good,' commented Tom.

'And it's real, so real that He made it human. He loves because it is His nature to love; there can be nothing un-loving about Him.'

Tom wanted to argue about so many of the world's problems but he remained silent. For years he had heard sermons about the love of God and still he had no idea of the nature of that love.

'Anybody who yields his life into the Father's hands puts himself into the hands of love, and the Father lovingly places him in Jesus,' Martin continued. 'God lovingly places him in Love. St. Paul expresses the nature of that love beautifully. "Love is patient and kind; love is not jealous or boastful; it is not arrogant or rude. Love does not insist on its own way; it is not irritable or resentful; it does not rejoice at wrong, but rejoices in the right. Love bears all things, believes all things, hopes all things, endures all things. Love never ends." '

'So different from the way I love,' thought Tom.

'It is into that kind of love that the Father places us. Do you realise the implications of that, Tom? You no longer have to live in the weakness of your own human love; you can live in the power of God's love.'

Tom wanted that kind of love; the poverty of his own was so obvious.

'God is a good Gardener, Tom, a very good Gardener. The Vine you have been reading about is to be an expression of what He is Himself. Because the Father is love, the Vine is to be a physical expression of that love, continuing the ministry of Jesus in the world.'

'You can conceive of such a love,' said Tom, 'but you can't see it. Such love doesn't exist in reality—it couldn't, or everyone would want it.'

'People may want it once they hear of it—but do they want it enough to pay the price?' Tom was aware of Martin's eyes on him.

'You can't buy God's love,' he countered.

'No, God gives freely—but not until we give ourselves freely to Him. He can't fill our cup until we realise it is empty and give it to Him.'

'I can see that,' said Tom, 'but how do I give myself, and what happens afterwards?' By now he had forgotten that he was talking to a hitch-hiker he didn't know and probably wouldn't meet again. For the moment Martin was to him the provider of the knowledge he desperately needed, and he clung on for all he was worth. Martin felt love being drawn out of himself, and yet he was filled with more and more warmth for this man whom he had to lead so carefully. He had never been so aware of being a channel of God's love, one link in the chain which would eventually bind Tom to his God. Martin felt like singing, but Tom's question was still unanswered, and it was as broad and far-reaching a question as he could have asked.

'Help me, Lord,' breathed Martin and reached for his Bible.

'Let's see what answer we can get from John 15, shall we? I think verse 2 gives us a pretty clear idea of what the Vine is all about. Listen. "Every branch of mine that bears no fruit, he takes away, and every branch that does bear fruit he prunes, that it may be more fruitful still." '

'A vine has a simple purpose: to bear fruit. It isn't an ornamental plant and it is no place for anyone who desires only a cosy, comfortable life, or who wants to retreat from responsibility. Such a person only draws life out of the rest of the plant and yields nothing. So there is little point in asking the Father to graft him into Jesus unless he intends to be productive.'

'So the initial down payment is the handing over of your life to God with the intent of being a productive branch of the Vine.'

Tom was pinning ideas down and analysing hard. 'Once I've handed my life over to God, I should start bearing fruit. What does that mean?'

' "The fruit of the Spirit",' quoted Martin, ' "is love, joy, peace, patience, kindness, goodness, faithfulness, gentleness, self-control".'

'Wow! Could you repeat that—but slowly. I just can't take it in.' Tom listened carefully, but it sounded even more of a tall order the second time round, and his mind was reeling. 'These are all the things I have needed for years, and when I've tried to achieve them, I've failed. I allow people to irritate me so that I can reject them, and then I hate myself and lose my peace. How is any of that going to change?'

'Listen once more, Tom. The verse begins "The fruit of the Spirit is . . ." The Spirit flows like sap through the whole Vine, and it is through the Spirit alone that we are productive. This is why we need to be grafted into Him: to allow the Spirit of God to flow continuously through us. Bearing fruit is a direct result of that, and not of any effort we might make.'

'It just turns upside down everything my life is based on,' said Tom. 'Here I am then, allowing the Spirit to produce fruit in my life—what about the pruning? What does that involve?'

Martin smiled gently, sensing the undercurrent of anxiety beneath Tom's analytical approach.

'God will want to deal with your sadness, anxiety, impatience, unkindness, faithlessness and so on. To do that effectively, He wants to bring you to the point of accepting, willingly, His pruning knife in your life.'

'Ouch! I feel like someone facing an operation.'

'The Master Surgeon will perform it personally; so you will be quite safe.' Martin was sensitive to the conflict going on within Tom. 'You need to believe that and not wriggle under the knife, or you will cause yourself pain instead of avoiding it. Anyway, only the bad or useless parts are going to be cut away, like part of your body which is making you ill. The alternative to facing the operation is death.' Tom winced.

'That's putting it rather strongly, isn't it?'

'Not really. Your life without God is only a gradual process towards death.' For a moment Tom was silent.

'Whereas in the Vine . . . ?' he queried.

'You become more and more alive with the life of God's Spirit,' finished Martin.

Tom drove on for a few minutes, and then, seeing a service area signposted, suggested a cup of coffee. He was almost dizzy with ideas, and needed a break from the driving as well. It was quite a relief to switch off the engine and still the droning. Tom went to wash and then joined Martin in the cafeteria, already fresher in mind and body. He had also had time to frame his next question.

'If I become a branch in the Vine of Jesus, what changes will take place in me?'

'There is no one answer to that,' replied Martin, 'because we are all individuals and God treats us as such. Most people experience a new love and joy, and a deep sense of peace that comes from living in harmony with God. This means worship will come alive, and prayer will have meaning and purpose, because you know the One you are communicating with, and know He can act.'

'I must admit I am horrified to see how many aspects of my life are going to have to change,' said Tom. 'Am I always going to be in a state of upheaval?'

'May I suggest, Tom, that most of your present state of disorientation comes from the indecision in your mind? "Do I dare take the plunge? In what ways is God going to change my life, my personality, my attitudes? How will my family and other relationships be affected?" The questions are mingled with a good deal of fear, and there is also the consciousness of your sin and failure in the past. All in all, there is quite a lot going on inside you!'

'Including the knowledge of my need to get back on the road again.' Tom smiled, and started off back for the car.

A few minutes later they were moving smoothly along in the fast lane and Tom could switch his mind to 'automatic drive' while he grappled with eternal verities.

'One problem which occurs to me is how to make the decision,' he admitted. 'A detailed mental analysis of God doesn't help me to love Him. Where can I start?'

'As you say, intellect can only take you part of the way. After that, your heart and will come into action. Then, once you have committed yourself, your intelligence can be used by God to help you discover things you would never have seen without Him.'

'So I need to give God my intellect as well?' Tom almost sighed.

'What better way to discover you trust somebody than to follow them on a path you don't understand?' argued Martin. 'There may be many occasions in the future when you won't understand, and then you will have to choose: either accept the situation as from God, or decide He has lost control, and take over the reins yourself.'

'It must be difficult to decide sometimes.'

'Yes Tom, very difficult. But the purpose of pruning is to cut away evil, not cause it. The Father has a very positive approach. He wants us to manifest more of His love, so He faces us with a situation in which we feel totally incapable of love. Once we acknowledge the fact that we can't love, God may show us that we didn't want to get too involved, or that we were afraid of our love being rejected. This recognition brings us to repentance so that we can be forgiven, and given the strength to grow in love and so bear more fruit.'

'So what may appear negative to us, is in fact positive in God's terms,' Tom concluded.

'Right,' said his passenger. 'Yet so many Christians grumble and moan when put to the test, and so fail to meet the challenge and grow. Instead, they harbour resentment against God for allowing something to happen to them, or for allowing a problem to remain.'

Tom felt there was much more to be said on this point, but they had reached the place where he had to turn off the motorway and leave Martin to find another lift.

'I can't tell you what our conversation has meant to me,' he said as he pulled into a layby on an approach road.

'I just hope I haven't made it sound too complicated,' said Martin. 'It would perhaps be better if you just remembered how God brought us together—but keep working at John 15. You've hardly started yet! God bless you, Tom.'

'I feel sure He will,' Tom replied. 'Goodbye, and thank you again.' The next few minutes required concentration as he found his way to the office block to meet his appointment. He made it with three minutes to spare.

'Mr. Billings?' the attractive receptionist said. 'Oh, yes Follow me. Have you had a good journey?'

How could he answer a question like that?

3

IT HAD BEEN a long day. Ann had felt condemned to solitary confinement. The persistent rain did not encourage any shopping expedition; she had no contact with her neighbours; and Ruth, her only close friend, had obviously gone out for the day. She tried to break the monotonous silence by turning on the radio, but soon became bored by the banal comments of the disc-jockey and the tedious repetition of the same records, most of which only seemed to emphasise her feelings of emptiness.

It was on days like this that she was thankful that Tony was not yet at school. He had returned from playgroup and had played quietly with his model cars for most of the afternoon, leaving her to do the ironing with only her own thoughts for company.

The sound of the telephone made her jump. 'At last! Contact with the outside world,' she thought as she made her way around the ironing-board to answer it.

'Ann Billings,' she said correctly.

'Hello, darling, it's me.'

'Tom!' Two calls in one day? It was more than she had received from him in the past month. 'I was just thinking about you.'

'What were you thinking?' he asked.

'I was wondering if you really meant what you said to me this morning; about telling me what's going on in you, I mean.'

'Of course I meant it. Listen. This is long-distance. You'll never guess. I've won the contract. At least, it was given to me. It's all very strange; but then some very odd things have happened to me today. I thought you'd like to know—about the contract, I mean.'

'Tom, that's wonderful.' Ann was delighted at the excited tone of his voice—more like the Tom she used to know, full of enthusiasm and expectancy. 'I'd still like to hear about the other things, though.'

'Yes, of course, darling. I'm coming straight home.'

'I'll have dinner in the oven then,' Ann replied quickly as the pips began. 'Drive carefully.'

'I will. 'Bye love. God bless you.' The line went dead.

36

'It would be difficult to know who was more surprised by the last phrase, Tom who spoke it, or Ann who heard it. 'God bless you too,' she said without much reverence and knowing full well that her husband couldn't hear. The words were immediately followed by the thought, 'I do hope he's all right.'

She had no more time to think about the matter, as the back door crashed open to announce that a very wet Angela had returned from school, eager to communicate the days' happenings to Mum. 'Just go and change those wet things first,' Ann insisted, 'then you can come and talk to me while I cook supper.'

'He's never said that to me before,' she reflected as she searched for chops in the freezer.

The drive home had been lonely. Tom had half expected to meet another friend, find another hitch-hiker. Anything seemed possible now.

'You're being stupid,' he told himself. Finally, he settled back, resigned to the fact that he was supposed to travel alone. It gave him time to reflect on all that was said that morning and upon the unlikely events of the afternoon.

It was late by the time he returned home, feeling physically tired, yet inwardly elated. He couldn't determine whether or not this was due to winning the contract. However, he longed to see Ann and talk to her—a longing that had been missing from his life for some time.

Tony was asleep and Angela was reading in bed, hoping for a good-night kiss.

'Hello, Daddy.' She greeted him with a hug as he bent over to kiss her. Tom sat on the bed.

'Angela, my sweet, have you had a good day?' He listened to the happy chatter about the teacher's eccentricities and friends' good-humoured jokes.

37

'It's time you were asleep. You have to go to school again in the morning.' While he was speaking Tom was making a mental note that he must spend more time with Angela, just talking with her. She would soon be grown up and he would have missed the joy of knowing his little girl.

'Angela, I think you are old enough to begin saying your prayers before you go to sleep.' She looked at him strangely. The Sunday service had been a natural routine in life, but what happened at St. Gabby's (as she always referred to it) was never brought into the home. It was always the drag before the enjoyable part of Sunday.

'What do I say?' she asked simply.

'Say thank you to your heavenly Father for all His love.' The ready way in which the words came to his lips surprised him.

Willing to be obedient, Angela closed her eyes and said, 'Thank you, God, for a lovely day. Amen.' She looked enquiringly at her father. 'Is that all right?'

'Well, He is your Father, not just God,' Tom replied.

'You are my father,' protested Angela.

'Yes, I am your earthly father and God is your heavenly Father,' explained Tom.

'Oh!' replied Angela. 'But I don't know Him. How can he be my Father if I don't know Him?'

'Precisely!' said Tom triumphantly. 'You need to know Him!'

'How?' The question was too simple for comfort.

'I'm not sure, Angela, but I'm going to find out.'

'Do you know Him, Daddy?'

'I'm beginning to. Yes, I really am beginning to. Come on, you must go to sleep. One day soon I'll tell you how you can know your heavenly Father.'

'I hope He's as nice as you, Daddy,' she said with a smile.

'You need have no fears about that; He's much nicer than I am. He's the perfect daddy.'

'You are, nearly,' Angela replied with a grin.

'I wish I was,' said Tom. He switched off the bedside lamp and turned to leave the room. He was surprised to see Ann standing in the doorway.

'I didn't hear you,' he said with obvious embarrassment.

'Tom Billings, I think you and I had better have quite a long talk tonight.' It was almost a threat.

'Let's enjoy dinner first,' he suggested.

'Tell me about the contract,' Ann said as soon as they had sat down. She had only just stopped herself from suggesting that they should say grace. The joke would have been in bad taste and she was none too certain of Tom's reaction in his present strange mood.

Tom helped himself to the runner beans in silence and then looked up at Ann. Her face was full of enquiry and her eyes seemed larger than usual, as if she were trying to pierce his mind with them.

'I've told you about Hanson before,' he began. 'Officious, correct, business-like; never gives anything away to anyone. Why should he, in a position like his? It was a long shot even attempting to obtain such a contract from him. It's much bigger than anything we've attempted before, and people like Hanson usually need ample proof of your ability to handle large contracts before they dish them out.'

He paused while he chewed a mouthful of chop and vegetables.

'The strange thing was that I wasn't frightened of him as I usually am, and when I was shown into his room he seemed genuinely pleased to see me. He was so civil and polite, charming even.'

'A business-man's ploy?' suggested Ann.

39

'No, no,' replied Tom, 'it was nothing like that. He seemed to be reacting differently towards me because I was different. I am different, Ann. I feel different.'

'In what way?' she asked.

'I don't know,' admitted Tom. 'I really don't know. That's the problem; I don't understand what's happening. It seems that I'm being drawn in a particular direction despite myself—like a nail attracted to a magnet.'

'And who is the attraction?' asked Ann. That same cold fear, irrational but real, prompted the remark.

'God,' answered Tom simply and devoted his attention to his dinner. He dared not look up for some time. When he did, he saw Ann watching him, her meal untouched. Their eyes met.

'Tom, you're not feeling ill, are you?'

He reached for his brief-case and searched for the contract. He opened the document and threw it casually on the table. Ann glanced down at the closely-typed page, her eyes focusing on the two signatures at the bottom.

'I'm not ill, Ann. In fact, I'm just beginning to realise that I've never felt better.'

With that he ignored her troubled gaze and concentrated on his meal; he had eaten little all day. Ann could only peck at her food. To say that she felt perplexed would be an understatement, yet it was some time before she put the obvious question. 'And what has the contract to do with God, Tom?' The tone was different; no longer were the words a challenge, more of an enquiry.

'I don't know the answer to that either,' admitted Tom. 'I suppose I'd better tell you the whole story. My meeting with Hanson is only a small part of what has happened in the last twenty-four hours. Is there anything else to eat?'

'There's fruit pie in the oven. I'll fetch you some,' said Ann.

'Finish your meal first,' suggested Tom.

'I'm not hungry, thanks.'

Ann went out to the kitchen with the dirty plates, unable to hold back the tears. She wiped her face on her apron and didn't see Tom come up behind her. He placed his arms around her and held her firmly. She needed that, the security of knowing that he really cared. Yet still she was totally unprepared for what followed.

'Ann, please forgive me.' Again that cold chill inside her. This time she prevented herself from saying anything. 'I know I've hurt you with my coldness and my indifference. I've been living behind a shield. I've snapped at you when I haven't intended to; I've been so wrapped up in myself that I've felt totally incapable of reaching out to you even when I've known you've needed me. I simply didn't dare face the fact that anybody needed me, because I've felt such a total, inadequate failure. I've avoided the children because I've felt I had nothing to give them. Ann, my darling, I'm sorry.' He kissed her lightly on the side of her neck.

'Oh Tom, why couldn't you have said all this long ago? I would have understood.'

'Because I couldn't face my insecurity until I had found the answer to it,' he replied.

'And you have found the answer?'

'I think so.' He deliberately did not slacken his hold on her, sensing that she might want to draw away from him.

'You had better tell me about this God, if He can make you that secure,' she said.

'First I want a kiss and my apple pie,' he countered.

'I've failed again,' said Ann. 'It's cherry.'

It had been many months since they had embraced with such meaning. For so long now their kisses had been routine. Whenever Ann had tried to express any tenderness to him, he had resented the interruption of his privacy and train of thought. If, at the end of the day, he had turned his attention to her at last, she would see this as a calculated prelude to going to bed, and dismiss it as meaningless. Now they relaxed, and each received gratefully what the other gave. The sensation was so new and glorious that their reaction was one of laughter.

'The cherry pie,' she said as they laughed happily.

'I'll go and change while you serve it,' said Tom.

Ann cut two generous portions. Her appetite had returned. She lamented the fact that there was no cream in the fridge; it would have been good to give Tom a treat. Never mind. He preferred ground coffee to the instant variety, so she set about measuring it out for the percolator. How strange that a simple embrace and a kiss could mean so much!

She was sitting in the lounge by the time Tom came downstairs, the pie and coffee on the occasional table. He slumped into a chair with a great sigh. 'Oh, that's good. That's very good—and the coffee smells delicious.' He smiled across at her. 'I was going to finish the story about the contract, wasn't I?'

'Never mind the contract!' retorted Ann. 'Let's have the whole thing, including God.'

Tom began with the description of his feelings on the previous evening and the meeting with his unexpected guest. Ann identified with many of the things that he said —the emptiness and the solitary feelings—and she began to understand the reasons for some of his moods. She had often blamed herself for these, and wondered if she was the cause of his withdrawal. Now she knew there was a deeper emptiness in Tom than she would ever be capable of filling.

The events of that morning seemed incredible, from the

meeting with Martin to the fact that Hanson had already drawn up the contract ready for Tom's signature. Obviously, these things had made a deep impression on her husband.

'I was disappointed that Martin wasn't around for the journey home. I wanted to thank him. Then it seemed that somewhere inside me a voice said, "Thank God". So I did. I began to thank Him; for Alan and Martin, the contract, for you and the children. I felt so happy that I even began to sing—you know, the good old hymns like "Praise my soul the King of Heaven". Somehow the words meant something. It wasn't like singing hymns in church; now I could identify with the words.'

'What do you think has happened to you?' asked Ann.

'I haven't the remotest idea what you would call it,' admitted Tom, 'but I like it. I just sang and sang and sang.'

'You didn't need anyone else?'

'No, I could thank God directly myself.'

'Where do you think we go from here?' asked Ann. She would welcome meeting somebody, as Tom had.

'I don't know yet,' answered Tom. 'Somehow I'm sure this isn't a dead end. I know I need revelation and I need a great deal more than I have so far received. There are still hundreds of questions to be answered.'

'Tell me,' said Ann. 'Did you begin to sing and feel happy before or after you had thanked God?'

Tom thought for a moment. This could be important; Ann had the habit of putting her finger on vital points like this. 'Afterwards. Yes, definitely afterwards. I was pleased about the contract, of course, but in a disbelieving kind of way. I could hardly believe it had happened. It was only after I thanked God that I felt so full of joy.'

'Why did you ask me to forgive you, Tom? You have never found it easy to apologise.'

43

'It was that same inner prompting that told me to thank God. I simply knew that I had to ask you to forgive me; that it was very important that you did forgive me. You do, don't you?'

'Of course I do, silly.'

Tom smiled and sipped his coffee. 'It was the same thing with Angela. I knew that it was right that she should pray and thank God.'

'Father.'

'Father?'

'You told her to thank her heavenly Father,' Ann reminded him.

'Yes, He is. He is my Father.'

'How do you know that?'

'I'm not sure. I just know it. In the car, when I couldn't think of anything else to thank Him for, I found myself saying "Father, Father, Father" over and over again. I know that God is my Father.'

'Is He my Father too?'

'Well, I suppose so, but perhaps you don't recognise Him as such yet. Don't ask me too many questions. I'm pretty new to all this.'

'Am I to thank God too?'

'You are big enough and old enough to make your own decisions, my love. I can't make that one for you.'

'Just as neither of your friends could make it for you.'

'I suppose so. You can't do something as big as that until you're ready.'

'You prayed last night, didn't you?'

Tom looked up at Ann abruptly. He had been so caught up with the day's events that he had forgotten that moment of anguish and despair: 'God, make me part of the Vine.'

'Yes, that's it. He's done it, bless Him. He's done it. He's made me part of the Vine.' Tom jumped up and began pacing up and down the room excitedly. 'You know what that means, don't you, darling? He's accepted me. Rotten old me. He's forgiven me; He hasn't rejected me. He really does love me.' Tom's face could not conceal the joy he felt.

'I love you, Tom, and I accept you just as you are.' Ann was close to tears.

Tom came over to comfort her. 'Darling, all this is for you as well as me. I know you love me. It's just that it's great to know that God loves me as well.'

'I need to know He loves me,' said Ann as she wiped her eyes.

'Of course He does,' insisted Tom.

'It's no good you telling me that. I have to know it for myself, just like you. And I don't have any stranger to help me.'

'You have me,' said Tom tenderly.

She grabbed hold of his hand. 'Tom, I know I have your love. This evening is the first time I have really felt that for months. Let me enjoy that and leave me to seek this other love for myself. I don't know how to love God or let Him love me, and I can't thank Him for that love until I'm sure of it. If there is a God, Tom, I thank Him for you. That's as far as I can go.'

The picture of Alan, quiet and patient, flashed into Tom's mind. He knew that he must not ask anything of Ann that she was unable or unwilling to give.

It was late. Tom pulled Ann to her feet. They could look forward to a deeper union with God and with one another in the future. Tonight they would enjoy that union of love that God had already given them and that they had not found satisfying for so long.

The dirty coffee-cups could wait until the morning.

4

THE CONGRATULATIONS FROM colleagues over the winning of the contract meant remarkably little to Tom. It seemed to him that he was being praised for something that had come as a gift. Besides which, he found to his astonishment there were more exciting things in life than work, ambition and prestige. He would have found it difficult to believe anyone who described the Holy Bible as an adventure, but that was precisely what it seemed to him now. Ann was already accustomed to the new sight of her husband reading avidly the pages of the New Testament every evening, and his frequent exclamations of 'Listen to this!'

She seldom made any comment on the words he read, sometimes because they meant nothing to her and she felt left out of Tom's world, sometimes because they struck home and niggled at her. Many of her long-held values seemed to be threatened and a sense of disorientation set in. Tom, on the other hand, was gripped by a new enthusiasm for life. He tried to share this with her, but that seemed to alienate her even further.

She didn't understand his confidence that God had grafted him into Jesus, and she couldn't always share his enthusiasm for the Bible, although she was impressed by his new concern for others, including herself. In fact, she was more aware of the improvement than was Tom himself, who was discovering just how difficult it was to overcome his pride, arrogance or jealousy. As he saw it, the Holy Spirit was pointing out his failures, and the Father was beginning to prune him.

The car was being serviced and Tom was making his way home by means of public transport. The wait at the bus stop seemed endless.

'When God speaks, His words do not return to Him empty: they accomplish what they were spoken to achieve.'

Tom turned round quickly. Alan gave a wide smile. 'Isaiah, chapter 55, verse 11,' he said.

It had been several weeks since their first meeting. 'Alan!' Tom blurted out and flung his arms round the man, much to the surprise of others in the queue. He didn't know how else to express his gratitude to his friend, and was lost for words. Having people around made this worse so he suggested they walk through a nearby park which would take them both in the right direction.

'How are you enjoying your new life in the Vine?' One look at Tom provided an answer, so Alan asked how St. Gabriel's was getting on.

'Very much the same for everyone else—but totally different for me,' replied Tom. 'I find I don't understand enough to explain to the rector, or even to Ann, but it's so real. The Bible has come alive, and the Spirit uses it to point out where I go wrong and what I can do about it. Yet I don't feel victimised—on the contrary there is a new sense of freedom, and I just want to work harder and harder at clearing out my life.'

'That sounds a very healthy state of affairs,' enthused Alan. 'So far you have been able to keep pace with God's purpose for you, and that is exhilarating, isn't it? This often happens to young Christians, to allow the graft to "take" properly. But I warn you that the time will come when God may ask more of you than you expected, or it may seem that He disappears and becomes remote.'

'I'd better keep an eye on Him then.' Tom smiled at the idea. 'Not that I had any intention of doing otherwise. But what should I do if it does happen? Forewarned is obviously forearmed.'

'Stick close to Him by the same means as you found Him in the first place,' answered Alan after a pause. 'That is, go on giving yourself with no thought of self.'

'With no thought of self,' repeated Tom. 'Hm. I suppose thinking of how I am improving or the next step I have to take verges on that.'

'It does indeed.' Alan was emphatic. 'Think of your attitude to worship. Have you ever been lost in praise in the church service and then *realised* that you are lost in praise, that you are singing louder, or praying longer?'

'Goodness, yes! You're quite right—the joy bursts instantly.'

'Because you have stopped giving yourself,' Alan continued. 'As soon as your eyes turn back on yourself, or you begin thinking about what you might get back, Jesus disappears from view.' The men walked on in silence while Tom digested this thought and saw God's logic behind it. By the time he spoke again his mind had moved on.

'When you have already given your life to God, what can you give next? I mean, it can't be totally repetitive —growth is an ongoing process.'

'It should be, Tom, although many people cannot accept the reality of the first stage and so never move any further. Yet Jesus calls us to action, has a definite plan for us, as He had for the first disciples. "Follow me," He said, "and

I will make you fishers of men." We cannot remain static. What about Paul—he certainly had the right idea. "One thing I do, forgetting what lies behind and straining forward to what lies ahead, I press on towards the goal for the prize of the upward call of God in Christ Jesus." '

Tom had been very happy to receive all that God had given him freely in the past weeks. He hadn't stopped to consider what the Lord might be asking of him, beyond a little pruning of certain aspects of his character. Yet he could see quite clearly now that he would soon be turning in circles unless he was careful; and that could not be God's way.

'What you have been experiencing so far is the heady sensation of the grafting and of the sap of the Spirit moving for the first time. This will continue as you allow God into more and more areas of your life. But He will also lead you into the understanding of many other passages of Scripture, many different aspects of His character, and you can't expect to remain untouched by this treatment. You will see not only God's promises, but also His demands. God desires that you bless Him, not only with your lips, but by giving your life freely for the good of His kingdom.'

'What is all this going to mean in practical terms?' Tom was feeling that a major upheaval was on the way, and there was apprehension in his voice.

'You will have to allow God to reveal that to you Himself. What is important now is that you grasp the principle and make the necessary response. Then God will be free to show you His purpose.'

'The principle being that I live to bless God, and allow Him to do with my life exactly as He pleases.'

'Tom, I can't help praising God for the way He is already at work within you.' Alan's admiration was genuine.

'The time for praising Him will be when I have responded in the way He desires.' Tom thought he had succeeded in correcting his friend at last.

'No, Tom; it is always the right time to praise God—now, and when you have obeyed Him.'

The introduction of the word 'obey' didn't escape Tom's attention. 'I thought God did not compel us,' he said.

'He does not compel, but He does command.'

'So disobedience is a possibility at any moment,' commented Tom.

'Sadly, yes. Once in the Vine, the branch needs to discover rapidly that it has to conform to the life pattern of the whole Vine. It can no longer wilfully go its own way. Some submit to that fact, because their desire is to be fruitful branches that will live for the glory of God. Others haven't passed the point of self-concern. They don't truly care about God's purpose for them. They are concerned only for themselves and what they can gain personally from the life of the Vine. God knows the heart and intentions of every man: no one can deceive Him.'

'I don't want to deceive Him.'

'I know that, Tom, and the Lord loves you for it. He rejoices in you and in the pruning you have already allowed Him to do. But every branch must expect continual pruning; then each harvest will be richer than the last.'

By now, Tom was getting used to the vocabulary Alan used, and was not put off by a tone that before he would certainly have described as pompous. He saw through that to the message, and the message was all too clear.

'Many Christians like to think of the fruitful times as the good times,' warned Alan. 'It seems that they are in harmony with God, their lives are filled with peace and joy, and they see Him using them to bring blessing into the lives of other people. But that fruitfulness is the result of all that God has done previously in their lives; it is the culmination of the growth that follows pruning. He will not be content with that: He will be looking forward to the next harvest when they will be an even greater blessing to Him and to others.

'It's no use pleading with the Father to leave us alone. We can't say "Let me stay at this level of productivity—I was pretty good last year; I want to rest this year." Look at that flower over there.' Tom's eyes followed the direction of the other's finger. A single bloom stood out among a sea of buds. 'That flower couldn't have produced itself; it is the natural result of the growth of the whole plant. In the same way, you don't have to become anxious about whether you are being productive enough to remain in the Vine. "Abide in me and I in you," says Jesus. If you do that, you will be fruitful.'

Tom admired the flower. It drew attention to itself simply because of its beauty. It couldn't speak. A prayer formed in Tom's mind: 'Lord, make me something beautiful in your sight, that I may live only for you.'

Alan noticed his silence and looked enquiringly at him. 'I have asked you to take in a great deal in a short time, Tom. Perhaps I'd better stop.'

'No, please,' said Tom. 'Please continue. I can follow what you're saying quite clearly.'

'Then I had better stop before I confuse you. Anyway, you aren't far from home now, and I turn down here.' The man stopped on the corner.

'Won't you come home and meet Ann? asked Tom.

'Not this evening, I think. There will be other opportunities. Can I just say that whenever you are conscious of God's pruning, you can know God's hand is upon you, even if you don't understand the necessity for what He is doing in your life. Be patient, for in time you will be given understanding.'

51

Alan stopped abruptly. 'I've been talking long enough and it's time I was going. The Lord bless you.'

Was Alan warning him of something? Or was this sense of foreboding only Tom's imagination?

5

TOM WALKED THE short distance home with a good deal on his mind. Ann was not at the door as usual; no, of course, she hadn't heard the car arriving. He rang the bell and waited. No noise of feet along the corridor, children shouting a greeting; the house was still. She must have slipped out for something—but the shops were closed by now, surely? He fumbled in his brief-case for his keys, his mind full of vines and pruning, trying to absorb what Alan had said. He let himself in, dropped his case in the hall and made for the kitchen and a cup of tea.

He didn't look at the piece of paper on the table until he had filled the kettle—it looked like Ann's scrawl in pencil on anything to hand. He picked it up. 'Tony has had an accident. Come to the hospital immediately, Ann.'

Tom dropped the note and ran. Was the car back from the garage? Yes. Ann must have gone with the ambulance. It was twenty minutes' drive to the hospital—at six o'clock at night it took half an hour. The lack of detail in the message terrified him. He was frantic as he burst through

the swing doors and asked at Enquiries. A maze of corri-
dors, white doors all alike and then, at last, Ann.

'Tom!'

'Where is he?'

'In there. It's a head wound.'

'How bad?'

'They haven't told me.'

Ann clung to him, shivering with fear. About an houi
earlier, Tony was playing outside when she had heard a
scream. She had run out, seen Tony lying in a pool of
blood, and phoned for the ambulance. The other children
had left her alone with Tony; she had felt alone ever since.

'All we can do is sit and wait, I suppose.' They sat close,
but there was nothing to say. It wasn't real. It couldn't be.
Tom had no idea how long it was before the door opened.

The doctor looked grave. 'It's brain haemorrhage. We're
doing all we can.'

An unbelieving silence. Tom had risen to his feet. He
sat down again slowly.

'God, no!'

'I don't know if you believe in God, Mr. Billings, but if
you do, your son could do with your prayers.'

With that the doctor was gone. The words had come like
a whipcrack. 'If you believe in God . . .' Tom had not even
thought of praying. So much for his new-found faith. But
could prayer help?

He forced his mind back to Alan, to his Bible studies.
He couldn't focus on anything, but surely here was hope.
God responds to faith, he told himself. Resolutely he turned to his wife, who sat, ashen-faced, in a chair beside him in
the bare room. 'Ann, my love, we must pray.'

'Pray?' came Ann's retort. 'What has God got to do
with all this?' Her mind was full of fear, and she couldn't
think of anything else. The tears slid quietly down to the

corners of her mouth. 'Still, if you want to, go ahead. You're the expert.'

'We must do it together, Ann.' Tom spoke with great difficulty, forcing the words out.

'Why?'

'I don't know. I just sense that we must be together in this.'

'I can't, Tom.'

'But Tony's life is at stake.'

'Do you really think it will make any difference?' Ann looked challengingly straight into Tom's eyes. He thought for a moment, then he knew.

'Yes, Ann, it will make all the difference.'

'I only hope you're right.'

'I know I'm right.' His own confidence surprised him.

'Go on then, you pray. All I can say is "Amen".'

The problem was what to pray. There had never been a time like this before. What was it Alan had said? 'It is always the right time to praise God.' How could he praise God for this? Yet it was true: God is always worthy of praise.

Tom began slowly. He had never prayed aloud with anyone before and Ann's reluctance made it more difficult. He was very embarrassed, but he couldn't back out now. 'Lord, we praise you and we thank you.' Ann looked up sharply, about to protest, but the intensity of Tom's face deterred her. 'Father, we know that you love Tony and I believe you're going to heal him. I'm sorry for my lack of faith. Please forgive me.'

When Ann saw the tears rolling down his cheeks, she too closed her eyes and tried to participate in what Tom was doing.

'Dear Lord Jesus, you have healed so many. Please, please stop this haemorrhage in Tony's head.'

54

'Please, Lord,' Ann's words came out in a sob. 'Please, Lord.'

'Thank you, Father. Oh thank you, thank you,' Tom whispered. A great hope had soared from deep within him. He didn't know why, but he knew that God had heard Ann pray, and that He loved all of them. Surely everything would be all right now, somehow! He looked up at Ann who, although wiping her cheeks with a handkerchief, had her eyes on him, wanting to trust he was right, but not really daring to hope.

'How can you be so sure?' Had the words come from Ann or from himself? Tom clung on to what he knew.

'Thank you, Jesus, thank you.'

They sat in silence, holding hands, but each lost in a different surge of emotions. What was happening? What was real? Another timeless pause. Then the door opened again, and they turned expectantly to the nurse who quickly answered the question in their eyes.

'Mr. Cummings says the haemorrhage seems to have stopped. You can see Tony briefly.'

If Tom hadn't been at her side, Ann might well have fainted for the second time that day, but for a very different reason.

'Is he conscious?' asked Tom.

'That isn't very likely. Why not go and see for yourself?'

Tony lay motionless, his face pale. There was a younger doctor and a nurse in the side-ward, besides the consultant.

'Your prayers must have been very effective, Mr. Billings. I didn't think he stood much chance.'

'How is he?' asked Ann.

'Still very weak. There is a chance that he'll make it so long as he doesn't begin to haemorrhage again.'

'And the damage?' asked Tom. 'Will he be normal after all this?'

'Impossible to say at this stage. Perhaps you'd better keep praying. Now I think you should take your wife home; there's nothing more you can do here tonight. Telephone the hospital in the morning. Good night to you.'

'We will, Doctor,' Ann said deliberately as Cummings turned to check Tony's pulse rate.

'You will what, Mrs. Billings?'

'We will continue to pray.'

'In my profession, it isn't easy to believe in God. You see so much human suffering. But every now and again something like this happens, and I wonder. Good night.'

'Good night,' they replied together.

They walked down the hospital corridor towards the main entrance. Ann stopped in front of the direction board.

'Come with me,' she said to Tom.

'Where are we going?' he asked.

'Never you mind.'

They climbed the stairs to the second floor, and Ann turned purposefully down the corridor to the hospital chapel. 'Well, don't just stand there,' she said, holding the door open, 'come in. Anyone would think that I'd never been inside a church before, judging by your face. We do go together every Sunday—remember?'

'Yes, but . . .' started Tom.

'But what?'

'It doesn't matter now.'

There seemed to be a quiet confidence and determination that Tom had not often seen in his wife. The chapel was still and peaceful. There was nobody else there. Instead of sitting in one of the pews, Ann went straight up to the altar rail and knelt down. He followed her in growing amazement.

'Lord, I'm sorry.' Her voice sounded boldly and could have been heard in any part of the chapel. Tom was glad it was empty. 'I've doubted you and thought goodness knows what about you this afternoon. I want you to forgive me and I want to know you as my Father.'

Without ceremony she stood up and walked out of the chapel. 'Oh, thank you, Father,' Tom hastily said as he chased after her.

'What happened?' he asked as they walked downstairs.

'What do you mean, what happened? Nothing happened! Is anything supposed to happen?'

'Well, yes. No. I don't know.'

She linked her arm in his. 'Tom, I just know that our heavenly Father is looking after Tony.'

'Pruning may be painful, but if this is the fruit . . .' said Tom.

'What are you talking about, Tom Billings?'

'Later, dear. I'll tell you later. What I want now is a cup of tea.'

6

IT WAS PERHAPS the strangest evening of their married life. They sat on the sofa as usual, facing the television, but for once the screen was blank and they were quite oblivious of it. The sight of their son, pale and still in the hospital, was impressed on their minds, and yet, even as they remembered, instead of the panic they might have felt, there was peace.

'It really is going to be all right, isn't it?' Ann voiced their question and the answer in one sentence. Yes, they both knew it was.

'You've come a long way today,' said Tom. 'Your first reaction was to scream at God and blame Him for what had happened.'

'That was partly shock,' Ann tried to excuse herself. 'One minute Tony was playing happily in the garden with his friends; the next he was lying in a pool of blood on the ground. He is so young, and it seemed so cruel.'

Tom could sense that Ann needed a tug away from that frame of mind before it overcame her. 'Come on, Ann, it would be too easy to wallow all night and that wouldn't do anyone any good. Let's have some coffee and think positively about where we go from here.'

'Back to the Scriptures, I should think.' Ann accepted his challenge, albeit with difficulty. 'If our knowing God can help Tony in some way, it's the least we can do. Anyway, I've got a lot to learn.'

Tom slipped out, just pausing at the door to take in the sight of his wife sitting over an open Bible. He couldn't resist going back to kiss her on the forehead; then he made his way to the kitchen.

'It's very reassuring,' said Ann as he came back with the coffee, 'but all muddled up. You say something, and that will give me a starting point.' Tom was ready to oblige.

'It's this "abiding" business that I must sort out,' he began. 'Jesus says "Abide in me, and I in you." I really need to understand what that means. This evening I failed miserably to do it and I don't know why. But for that doctor asking me whether I believed in God it might never have occurred to me to pray.'

'We have no proof that the prayer stopped the haemorrhage,' said Ann.

'None at all,' agreed Tom. 'But remember, I knew Tony was going to be all right when we prayed, before the nurse came with the news that the bleeding had stopped.'

Again the shadow of fear was there. This was no academic point of doctrine; it was literally a matter of life and death. Yet the reality of the situation drove them back to doctrine for the real answers they needed. Tom had recently bought a concordance. He thumbed through it now, looking for the word 'abide'. He discovered that the Greek word usually translated in this way means 'to remain, to continue'.

'It seems that Jesus is really saying to His disciples, "Go on continuously living in me as I go on continuously living in you." '

'You believe your life has been given into the Father's hands?' Ann asked reflectively.

'I'm certain of that,' answered Tom; 'that's why everything has been so different during these past weeks. Your life is in His hands too.'

'Yes, I think that is true,' she agreed. 'I felt that is what I was doing in the chapel. Somehow, I knew God had proved Himself to me. It's funny, really; it's very difficult to put my finger on what was happening. I was sorry for my reaction earlier and for all that I had said about Him, and thought too, and I sensed that He had forgiven me. It was as if He was saying, "All right, Ann. Let's start again, together." So I thought, "Right Lord, here goes!" '

'So you stood up and walked out of the chapel,' suggested Tom.

'Yes, I thought I had better get on with it.'

'With what?' The question wasn't easy to answer.

'With this business of living with God, that you have

been on about for the last few weeks, I suppose.'

'I think you need to learn something about "abiding" too,' smiled Tom, 'but I know what you mean about forgiveness. I found a verse somewhere the other day which said that God promises to wash away our sins like a mist that dissolves away.'

'The Lord needs to do a lot more cleaning up inside me. I still have several foggy patches.' Ann seemed very thoughtful.

'Don't worry,' Tom reassured her. 'He will get round to all of them in time.'

Ann closed her eyes and could have been praying. Her thoughts needed to be private.

Tom thought about Alan's introduction of the word 'obey' into their conversation. For so long his Christian life, such as it was, had seemed to be a blind obedience to the injunction that he should worship every Sunday. Now that he had discovered the grace of God, he had been delivered from a legalistic approach to religion. Yet Jesus had plenty to say about obedience. 'If you love me, you will keep my commandments.' There was no escaping the Lord's meaning, although it was growing too late to find the answers to his many questions that night.

Ann had slipped into sleep, the strain of the afternoon's events being soothed away. She woke up just enough to get to bed and said nothing about the situation before drifting back to the sleep she needed so much. Yet Tom sensed she was at peace, and his last thought that night was of thanks to God that He knew their needs and was meeting them.

Early the next morning, Ann's first thought was for Tony. The picture of him lying in the hospital bed was as vivid as ever, but now it was accompanied by a prayer:

'Father, keep him safe.' She quietly slipped out of bed and dressed without disturbing Tom.

The house was uncommonly quiet. The usual noise of Tony playing in his room was painfully absent. He was always the first up in the Billings household and Ann was accustomed to waking to the sounds of a multiple model-car crash or Angela's protests at being disturbed by her young brother.

Although it was not yet seven o'clock, Ann could not refrain from telephoning the hospital. Tony was still on the critical list. The sister suggested that they delayed their arrival until after the doctor had seen Tony at around ten.

Ann was confused. She wanted to believe that this faith business was simple and straightforward. After all, Jesus had healed people instantly, but she didn't feel she had the right to expect that to happen with Tony. She made a cup of tea, and took it upstairs. She needed to talk and was relieved to find that Tom was already stirring.

'Hotel service!'

'How's Tony?' asked Tom.

'He had a comfortable night, but is still on the critical list.'

'Can we see him?'

'After ten, when Cummings has seen him again.'

Tom's thoughts were no clearer than Ann's. Suddenly, he sat up.

'Ann, answer me this!'

'What now?' she asked, startled, as she mopped some of the tea which had spilt on the sheet with the sudden movement.

'When we prayed for Tony last night, what did you expect would happen?'

'I don't know, quite. I suppose I hoped that God would

61

cure him, that he would regain consciousness and that there wouldn't be too much brain damage. Why?'

'It's something Jesus says about prayer.' Tom was thankful for the hours he had spent reading the Bible in recent weeks. Now he searched his mind hard to remember the words exactly. 'He says something like this: that if, when we pray, we really believe that what we are praying for will happen, then it will happen. If we believe that Tony will get better when we pray, then he will.'

'I see that,' said Ann, 'but how do you make yourself believe like that?'

Tom had no answer. He sipped his tea quietly. 'Let's see what we do believe,' he suggested. 'Do you believe that Tony will be cured?'

Ann didn't need to delay in her answer. 'Yes. Yesterday afternoon I couldn't have said that; now the answer is definitely "Yes".'

'When do you think he will be cured?' asked Tom. That was not so simple.

'I honestly don't know. One part of me wants to say it will be sudden, another part says it will be a long process. I suppose I really believe the second although I want to believe the first.'

'Me too,' admitted Tom.

'When you say that Tony will be cured, what do you mean by that? Do you think the healing will be perfect so that there is no brain damage?'

Ann thought for a very long minute. 'I must confess it had never occurred to me that the healing could be perfect. I took the doctor's word that there was bound to be some damage. I've just hoped that it would be as little as possible.'

'Perhaps if we believe there will be no damage, there will be none,' suggested Tom.

'Again, how do you make yourself believe that?' asked Ann sadly.

'I wish I knew.' Tom sighed. 'I really wish I knew.'

Tom again broke the silence. 'It shouldn't be like this.'

'It's impossible to understand why things like this happen,' replied Ann. 'We all have accidents, I suppose. The trouble is some turn out to be far more serious than others.'

'Yes,' he agreed, 'but I didn't mean that. It shouldn't be like this in the Church. The early Christians seemed to love and care for one another in a way that we never see now. What would happen if we took our problem to St. Gabriel's?'

'Dear Mr. Dean would go and see Tony. He is very good at hospital visiting. He would probably want to see us too.'

'And what would he say?'

'I really don't know, Tom. I've never been in a situation like this before.'

'Would he be able to answer our questions? Could he tell us how to believe in the way we need to believe?'

'There's only one way to find out.' Ann reached for the telephone and dialled the number of the rectory.

'It's very early to ring,' protested Tom weakly.

'Oh hello, rector. This is Ann Billings. I'm very sorry to phone so early, but we have a problem we would like you to help us with. Our little boy, Tony, is in hospital. He had some kind of accident yesterday. He has a fractured skull and was haemorrhaging badly. Thankfully the bleeding has stopped but he is still critically ill.'

Tom could faintly hear Mr. Dean's 'Oh dear, I am sorry' at the other end of the line. 'How can I help you?'

'Do you think we could call in to see you on our way to the hospital, at about 9.30? Oh, thank you. That will be fine. Good-bye and God bless you.'

63

Ann replaced the receiver and then realised what she had said. She looked at Tom and they both laughed. 'Am I allowed to bless rectors?' she asked.

'Well, you've just blessed that one.'

Mr. Dean's study showed the usual priestly problem. Piles of correspondence lay on his desk unattended, owing to the pressure of his pastoral responsibilities.

'I really am very sorry to hear about this,' he began. 'I shall go and see Tony myself later. I expect to be visiting in the hospital this afternoon. And we shall put him on the prayer list.'

'It's about prayer that we have come to see you,' said Tom. He outlined the conversation he had earlier that morning with Ann. The rector listened intently but said nothing. 'How can we make ourselves believe in the way we need to believe?' Tom concluded with the vital question.

The parish priest looked sad. 'You can't,' he said. 'For years I have been searching for that kind of faith myself and I haven't acquired it. Many times, I've wished for it because I have seen such need for it. Yet it has always eluded me.'

His honesty touched them both and created within them a concern for him rather than for their own problem. Suddenly he buried his face in his hands. Tom and Ann looked at one another, uncertain what to do. After a while, the rector's voice sounded muffled from behind his hands. 'I'm sorry; I don't know what's come over me. This is most unlike me.'

'Shall I call your wife?' suggested Ann.

'No, no, don't do that.' He seemed to recover a little at the suggestion. They sat in an awkward silence.

'Perhaps we'd better go to the hospital,' suggested Tom.

'Please, don't go just yet.' They couldn't ignore that plea. The rector, aged suddenly before their eyes, had lost his habitual dignity and charm. He fumbled at the papers on his desk as he spoke, and mumbled as though he were unsure of his voice.

'Time and time again, I have come to this point in my ministry,' he began. 'This is one time too many. You see, when I read the Bible, I come across so many things that we are told to do. I often want to do them, but I can't. I can't, because I haven't the power to do them. Jesus told His disciples to heal the sick and they did. They healed because He healed. I have never healed. For years I have seen sick people in their homes, in hospital; sometimes they are critically ill and are dying. I can do nothing for them except try to comfort them. I suppose I have become quite good at that, but it never satisfies me. When I go to see your boy, I shall see him lying there and I shall think, "Poor little mite." My prayer would be, "God, what a mess!" You see, Tom, I have reached a point of despair when it comes to sickness.'

'That's great!' Tom didn't mean to sound so enthusiastic. The rector looked up and gazed steadily at him. 'Don't laugh at me—please.'

'I'm not laughing,' assured Tom. Simply he related the events of the past few weeks, his own personal point of despair, and how he had come to know God as a result.

'I have seen this change in you recently. I must admit I have been envious at the way you have obviously been lost in prayer at the communion service. I don't think what you have said will help me, though, Tom. I met with God years ago; that is what led to me being ordained. It all seems like a dream from the past now. Somewhere along the line, I feel He left me behind.'

Tom was out of his depth. He hadn't come here to counsel the rector in his problems.

'I wish I knew the answers to give you,' he said. 'We are all so inadequate and powerless. Jesus empowered His first disciples to heal, so why shouldn't He empower us?'

'That is a question I have asked myself many times. I try to rationalise an answer by saying that now we have the medical profession and there are not the same needs as there were in a more primitive society. But that isn't the whole answer and I know it. The doctors have their limitations, and God is almighty. That means He has the power to do anything. Often I am tempted to think that He doesn't really want to heal. Yet I know that such a thought is inconsistent with the Jesus of the Gospels.' The priest shrugged his shoulders in a gesture of resignation and defeat. 'So I have to get on with the only thing I know, which is how to give comfort to those in trouble.'

'That is an important gift to have,' said Ann.

'Yes, my dear, it is important in some situations. It is a very poor second-best in others.'

'Like this one,' Tom suggested.

'Yes,' agreed Dean, 'like this one.'

Tom and Ann left the rectory with more unresolved questions burning within them. They could have done with an immediate answer on which to base their hope. Instead, they must go and hear the latest verdict from Dr. Cummings.

'He is holding his own. I can say no more. There is still no sign of consciousness, which is a pity. The longer he is unconscious the more chance there is of brain damage.' The consultant looked grave.

'You didn't really expect him to live last night, did you, Doctor?' Tom looked straight at him as he asked the question.

'Not when he first came into casualty; I must confess I didn't. There seemed a sudden change while you were here yesterday. One of those strange occurrences for which one can give no medical reason. Since then, young Tony's condition has remained static.'

Tom and Ann sat quietly for some minutes by Tony's bedside. There was no flicker of movement, except for slight evidence of his very shallow breathing. They tried to pray their confused thoughts, but with little sense of satisfaction. There seemed no point in remaining for long, so Tom suggested a cup of coffee in the hospital cafeteria.

'Perhaps we've been kidding ourselves,' suggested Ann. Within the atmosphere of the side-ward, it had been difficult to imagine that any sudden change could take place. Away from the situation, it had seemed easier; there in the hospital it was different.

'No, I don't think so. We simply need a few answers to some very direct questions.'

The cafeteria was crowded. Ann went to find two places at a table while Tom queued for the drinks. No tables were free, but one in the corner by the window had only a single occupant. Ann would have liked some privacy for her conversation with Tom, and was pleased that the man had nearly finished his drink. He looked up and smiled at her as she sat down and then returned to his book. Ann waved to Tom to indicate the direction in which to come. He was within six feet of the table when he recognised the figure.

'It's you again!'

The man looked up. 'Ah, Tom. Do come and join us. This, I take it, is Ann.' This time he not only smiled, but held out his hand.

'Darling, this is Alan.'

'How do you do?' said Alan briefly. 'How is Tony?'

'He is holding his own, but still critical,' Tom replied.

'How do you know about Tony?' Ann's voice had a challenging note.

'Oh, you know how news gets around offices and neighbourhoods. I felt I might be needed and was pretty sure of finding you here.' Ann was not quite satisfied by Alan's answer, but comforted by his presence.

'You are certainly needed,' agreed Tom. 'We have some questions to ask you. I'm not sure which is uppermost in my mind. Our need to believe that God can heal Tony completely, or the sight of a rector in tears because he can't help us.'

Ann was quite sure which was more important to her, and was a little annoyed when Alan started talking about the Church. It was several minutes before she began to listen to him.

'God does not see each branch in splendid isolation,' he was saying. 'To be part of the Vine is not only to live in Jesus but also to belong to one another. You see, unless the branch is securely grafted on to another branch, it will not continue to receive the life of the Vine. Jesus says, "A branch cannot bear fruit by itself."

'Can you imagine a branch floating about in space saying, "I have my personal relationship with God"?' Alan's eyes sparkled. 'Would you expect such a branch to receive life from the Vine? Branches separated from the Vine will be "gathered, thrown into the fire and burnt."' The last phrase made Ann suddenly react.

'But until recently I would have thought belonging to the other members of St. Gabriel's ridiculous. And I don't think they would want to be involved on that level either —not that I really know them very well.'

'We cannot share God's life and love with one another very freely if our relationships are formal or superficial,'

68

Alan pointed out. Ann smiled, recognising that they were basically on the same side. 'Do we really want to share our lives with each other at all?' she asked.

'Now that we've finished our drinks shall we go somewhere less crowded?' suggested Tom. Some of the benches in the hospital gardens were occupied by patients in dressing-gowns, enjoying the sunshine and the change from the atmosphere of the wards. Ann chose a vacant seat in the shade of a large oak tree. She hoped the subject would turn to Tony now, but Alan obviously had more to say about the Church.

'There are many people who either think only of producing their own fruit, or who want to know God better but miss out on the relationships with others that would help them so much in their spiritual lives. God's plan for the individual is worked out in the context of His purpose for the whole Church.'

'And yet what do you do, faced with a church like St. Gabriel's?' objected Tom. 'Our "life" there consists of Sunday services, money-raising functions, and the occasional Bible-study course which usually fails for lack of support.'

'It must have occurred to you, Tom, that the change in your lives could affect others in the church?'

Tom had thought of this, but to hear it stated aloud made him feel very inadequate. 'I seem powerless to bring about any change,' he said.

'But God is not powerless, Tom. In His mind there is the vision of what St. Gabriel's ought to be: a body of people who receive His life and love and power. They know how to share what they receive with one another and others who come seeking an answer to their needs.'

'When the church is as God wants, will He then provide

the power to heal people like Tony?' asked Ann, desperately wanting to relate all that was being said to the present predicament.

'No, Ann. If God waited for that, He would never release His power. Men will not become that kind of church if they attempt to do so in their own strength, only if their lives are first filled with God's life and power and love.'

'That's what we need,' blurted out Tom. 'God's power. That's what we need now.'

Alan smiled. 'Why? To heal Tony or to become the kind of church that God desires?' Tom took the point.

'Both,' he replied.

'Amen,' echoed Alan.

'But how do we receive this power?' continued Tom, his heart beating faster.

'Jesus said to His disciples, "You shall receive power when the Holy Spirit has come upon you." He knew that the Church would be unable to fulfil its purpose, that of continuing His ministry, without such a baptism of power.'

'I was baptised as a baby,' said Ann, 'but perhaps I've never understood what it meant.'

'It means that you have died,' said Alan.

Both she and Tom were puzzled now.

'Perhaps a verse from Romans would help. Paul says, "We were buried therefore with Him (Christ) by baptism into death, so that as Christ was raised from the dead by the glory of the Father we too might live in newness of life."'

'Then I'm not the person I was born?'

'And I must have an entirely new life.'

'Right, both of you' Alan laughed. 'Go to the top of the class. The old you is dead and buried, but you won't live in the power of the new one until you recognise that fact.'

'So what is the Holy Spirit? I thought I had received the

Holy Spirit when I was baptised and confirmed.' Ann was still perplexed.

'Who can say that it isn't the Holy Spirit given at that time who has led you to where you are today?' Alan smiled. 'I say "who", because the Holy Spirit is a person, not a thing; He is God. The Father loves us, the Son died for us, and the Holy Spirit is God alive within us. Does that help?'

But Ann hadn't heard Alan's neat summary of the Trinity—the words 'where you are today' had turned her thoughts back to Tony, and the theology had become irrelevant again.

'Oh God, help him.' Her face contorted. Alan put an arm firmly round her shoulders and produced a handkerchief. Now that she had given up the pretence of calm conversation, she was quite without resources against the pain and fear which blacked out her mind. Yet she gradually became aware of Alan's strength beside her and, with the perspective of his faith, hope returned. As her sobs subsided, she tried to apologise, but Alan rubbed her arm with affection.

'No, you are right to feel—details of doctrine don't meet your need. You understand enough to know the way forward, and Christ will teach you the rest as you go. You need to go to Him and ask to be baptised in power and love—to be baptised in the Holy Spirit of God.'

'But what do I say?'

'Tell Jesus that you are giving Him your life, and want to live for Him. Give Him your sins, your fears, your doubts. Give Him your character, your time, your loves; give Him everything. Give Him Tony and Angela and Tom.'

'Give him Tony? But what if He takes him?'

'He has the perfect right to do that. He is God.'

'I'm not sure I can face that.' Ann's voice cracked.

71

'Then tell Jesus how you feel.' Ann hesitated, even when she saw Tom stand up resolutely.

'I'm going to the chapel now.' He spoke and moved quietly, knowing that he must not influence her decision in any way. He wanted to touch her hand, to plead with her; it mattered so much that she should follow him. Slowly he walked across the grass, his eyes turned to the hospital and the chapel. It was a long way, and yet too near.

Suddenly her hand slipped into his.

'I'm coming too,' she said firmly.

7

WHEN THEY REACHED the chapel, Tom and Ann agreed to separate. They each had business to do with God and needed to be quite alone with Him. Ann was so eager to know God's presence that she quickly sat in a chair near the door, while Tom walked up to kneel at the altar rail. Yet their purpose was the same—to meet God.

And God came to them both as individuals, and they felt His love and goodness, beside which they knew themselves to be worthless. Both wept at the futility of their lives without Him, and asked Him to take them and make of them something new. Both prayed that Jesus would baptise them with His Holy Spirit.

To Ann this was a great surprise. She felt a great heat

pass through her body. It seemed that her face was on fire. Her arms opened spontaneously as if she were greeting her Lord. Momentarily she thought her heart would burst. She wanted to speak but could find no words to express the wonder of His presence. Then she found herself speaking strange words that seemed to flow naturally from deep inside her somewhere, words she couldn't understand but which expressed what she wanted and needed to say. For several minutes she was oblivious of her surroundings, 'lost in wonder, love and praise'.

'I love you, Father, I really love you. Jesus, thank you.'

For Tom, there was nothing of this. No excitement, no strange tongue, no sensation, nothing except an inner conviction that God was faithful and had honoured His promise. He knew that he had been given the power he needed to live in God's strength and not his own. He had already known God's forgiveness, that his life was in His hands. Now there was a greater certainty of the bond that existed between them: God and man. He was at peace. And as he prayed for Tony, he had the overwhelming conviction that God had the whole matter under control.

His only problem arose when he turned round to look at Ann. He felt a sharp pang of jealousy at the radiance of her face. The feeling intensified when she came forward, knelt beside him and hugged him.

'Oh Tom, He is wonderful. He just told me that you and I are going to have a very different life and that we mustn't fear, because He is going to lead us.'

Again the pang of jealousy. He hadn't heard God speaking. Then he realised that Ann had only voiced what he had inwardly felt. Perhaps the Lord had different ways of communicating with different people. He returned the hug.

'Will it always be as wonderful as this?' she asked. Her eyes were closed and she seemed lost in rapture. He didn't know what to say. Perhaps it was best that he said nothing.

'What about Tony?' he asked after a discreet pause.

'Goodness,' said Ann. 'I'd forgotten all about him. I was so busy loving God that nothing else seemed to matter!'

'Well, Tony matters.' Tom was finding this jealousy difficult to cope with.

'I know he does, silly. But with such a wonderful God, he's bound to be all right.'

He was thankful that she seemed oblivious of his problem as she almost skipped down the aisle of the small chapel and collided with Dr. Cummings as he came through the door.

'I thought I might find you here.'

Ann looked startled. 'I'm sorry. I just feel so excited and almost light-headed.'

'Excited?' He looked at her. 'If your eyes didn't sparkle in that way, Mrs. Billings, I might suggest a sedative.'

Ann had no time to ask him what he meant before Tom asked about Tony's condition.

'You must have been praying again. About half an hour ago he regained consciousness. The extraordinary thing is that he seems bright and alert.'

'There appears no sign of brain damage?' Tom asked.

'It's much too early to be certain of that. So far the signs are good, and certainly the damage is not as extensive as I had feared.'

'Can we see him?' asked Ann.

'For a few minutes. Please understand that I don't want him excited. The danger may not yet be over completely. There are a number of tests that will need to be carried out.'

They made their way to the ward quickly. Cummings grabbed Tom's arm before they opened the door. 'Remember what I said, please: no excitement.'

Tony had propped himself up in the bed and was trying to look out of the window.

'Now then, young man, you are supposed to be lying down quietly.' There was no chance of that when he saw Tom and Ann. It was a job to contain his enthusiasm—or theirs, for that matter. As they listened to his chatter they were surprised that he showed no signs of distress at his strange environment. Cummings was true to his word and quietly ushered them out after only five minutes.

'He seems fine,' said Ann with obvious relief.

'Well, Mrs. Billings, I must confess that I am surprised myself. There must be some medical explanation for this sudden improvement. I have invited one or two colleagues to come and examine him later today. It is a fascinating situation.'

'Well, don't get him too excited,' said Ann. They all laughed. The tension of the whole situation seemed to have drained away.

It was by now mid-afternoon. They had not felt hungry earlier in the morning and lunch had been far from their thoughts. They decided to go home and fix some omelettes. On the journey they found themselves singing, 'Now thank we all our God' at the top of their voices, careless of the stares from passers-by and other drivers when they stopped at the traffic lights. Their singing stopped abruptly when Tom swung the car on to the tarmac in front of their garage.

A woman rose hesitantly from the doorstep on which she had been sitting. Tom thought at first she was going to run away, until he saw she was drained of energy. Her puffy red eyes suggested someone who had cried through the night, and the uncombed hair was that of a woman who had given up.

'Rhona!' Ann suddenly recognised her and rushed forwards. Rhona Menzies was a neighbour whose younger son was roughly the same age as Tony.

'Rhona! Whatever is the matter?'

'Oh, Ann. I'm sorry. I am so sorry. He didn't mean it. I know he didn't mean it. How is he? Oh, the poor boy!' She collapsed into Ann's arms. Tom rushed to her assistance, thinking that he had seen more adult tears shed in the last twenty-four hours than in a lifetime.

'Bring her in,' he suggested.

Ann settled her on the sofa and tried to calm her sobs while Tom went to make some tea. It was some minutes before Rhona sat up straighter and blew her nose determinedly on Tom's handkerchief.

'Now tell me what's wrong, Rhona.'

'You mean you don't know?' The woman looked both startled and even more frightened at the possibility.

'Know what?'

She fumbled with her fingers, picking nervously at her nails.

'Please tell me, Rhona.' She sat silently. Tom came in with the tray of tea. The familiar warmth and taste seemed to help.

'It was Roger who did it. But he didn't mean to,' she added quickly. 'He didn't understand. I'm sorry. Really I'm sorry.' Again, they had to wait for the tears to subside. 'How is Tony?' she asked when she felt able to speak again.

'He's fine.'

Relief spread over Rhona's face. 'I thought he was dying. Mrs. Whittaker told me that there was little hope.'

'She was right,' said Tom, 'at the time. Now he's making a remarkable recovery.'

'Oh, that's wonderful. That's really wonderful. But I still feel so sorry that my Roger has caused all this.'

'Do you know what happened, then?' asked Ann. 'I couldn't make any sense out of the children yesterday, and was too concerned about Tony to worry very much.'

'Simon is a little older than the others and he told his mother, who phoned me. Apparently there is some wood stacked by your shed. Roger picked up a slat and started swinging round with it. He caught Tony a great crack on the side of the head.'

'I didn't see the wood in his hand—or lying on the ground for that matter.'

'He had the presence of mind to put it back where he found it. Obviously he felt guilty. I don't expect you to forgive us for causing you all this trouble, but truly I am sorry.'

'Listen, Rhona!' Tom's voice was crisp. 'Ann and I realise that it was an accident and even if Roger had done it deliberately, we would forgive him completely. We have no hard feelings towards him or you.'

Rhona looked a little happier. 'Thank goodness it wasn't more serious.'

This time Ann had the answer. 'Rhona, it doesn't matter how serious; it would have made no difference. We would forgive Roger just the same.'

She looked at Ann with utter disbelief. 'Don't be silly! You couldn't help being upset.'

'Upset, of course. But we would still have tried to forgive Roger or you or anyone else who had been responsible.'

'Why should you?'

'Because it never helps to hold on to bitterness or resentment. All of us need forgiveness. How can we expect to receive it if we aren't prepared to give it?'

Rhona looked pensive. 'How do you get it?'

'By asking God for it.' Tom spoke when Ann hesitated.

'What would He want with me? Still, I haven't come here to talk about myself. I'm so relieved that Tony is going to be all right. It's really wonderful what these doctors can do these days.' It was as if she had suddenly put on a mask, ashamed of what she had revealed already about herself. Tom and Ann looked at one another. Both were thinking that it would be better to let her go. Perhaps an opportunity would arise soon when they could show Rhona the way to forgiveness and a new life.

It was good to be home and they were tired. Tom kissed Ann lightly. 'Sit down and finish your tea. I'll do the omelettes.'

Three days later, Tony was the centre of a home-coming celebration. There was his favourite raspberry jelly with ice-cream, and fruit cake with nuts on the top. Angela had made a big poster which was sellotaped to the front door, saying simply, 'Welcome home, little brother.' Around the edge were matchstick doctors and nurses looking very busy and efficient.

Mr. Cummings had asked Tom and Ann to see him personally when they collected Tony from the hospital. Trying to be as scientifically detached as possible, he announced that a further X-ray had revealed that there was apparently no fracture after all, and that there was no sign of the scars normally left after a haemorrhage. When challenged further, he suggested that there must have been some mark on the previous X-ray plate, which had been interpreted as a fracture; however, he had to admit that he could not account for the absence of any internal scarring. 'That,' he said thoughtfully, 'is quite amazing.'

'Don't you believe in prayer?' Ann had asked him. To which the consultant replied that he had seen too many prayers go unanswered to understand the workings of the

Almighty. However, he was delighted for Ann and Tom and any others apparently in divine favour. Tom had wanted to say that anyone could be placed in that position by Jesus. Somehow the time didn't seem right. The waiting-room was full and Tony was eager to be home.

Vigilant to the last, Cummings warned them to watch him carefully for a few days and not to allow him to become involved in activities that were too boisterous or physically demanding. As they left, the doctor had a puzzled expression. When they had gone, he shivered, threw the file into the 'Out' tray and summoned the next patient.

Ann felt she had never experienced such happiness as in the three days before Tony came home. The housework was not the drudgery it had often been. She went around the house singing gaily. The words of many of the old hymns that she had sung mindlessly for years now took on new meaning. Without Tony at home, she had the opportunity to sit down and pray. It was as if the Lord stood in front of her and she could exult in His presence.

Occasionally, she questioned her sanity when she found herself singing or speaking in this strange language that came so readily to her lips. Such thoughts quickly passed away, however, in the sheer joy of knowing her unity with her heavenly Father through the praise within her. Tom had been a great help in showing her passages from the New Testament that not only validated this practice, but also encouraged it. 'If it was good enough for St. Paul, it's good enough for me,' was the cheerful conclusion she came to. Her one unspoken fear was that despite her gift she was failing to be fruitful.

Tom's attention at this time was focusing on the Vine as manifested in St. Gabriel's. On the evening before collecting Tony, Ann was rushing around trying to make the house tidy enough for him to mess up again, when Tom interrupted her.

'A vine has a consistent cycle of growth,' he said with the authority of matured consideration, 'culminating in the harvest of the fruit. The clusters of grapes should show a consistency of colour, ripeness, quality and taste. It seems to me that if Alan is correct and God is concerned with the health of the whole Vine, and not only of a few branches, then He desires to see this cycle of growth taking place in the whole of the Vine locally. He wants good, ripe fruit everywhere. He doesn't expect it to be ripe on one branch, sour on another, the colour of one branch rich, of another speckled and insipid.'

'That's certainly a clear way of putting it,' agreed Ann. Then, as her practical nature came to the fore, she added, 'But how are you going to bring it about? I see no sign of the congregation at St. Gabriel's knowing that life in Christ is possible, let alone wanting it enough to ask Him for it. Not even Christopher Dean.'

'Then surely it's up to us to show them what it is and how to get it,' reasoned Tom.

'But how can I explain what I don't understand myself?'

'That had me stumped for a while,' admitted Tom, 'and then I suddenly saw it quite clearly. There are many aspects of our new life which aren't so easy to put across, but the reason for it is very simple. Tell me, when did it all really start for you?'

'Well, in the chapel, I suppose.'

'And what did you do there?'

'I just saw my life in a new perspective. It wasn't enough to ask God to come into my inadequate life. I needed to acknowledge that I belonged completely to Him.'

'In one word then, Ann, you repented. Surely this is

exactly what God wants: that everyone in His Church should turn their lives over to Him. This is the keystone—repentance. And that doesn't just mean being sorry for your sins; it means handing over everything to God. If the whole congregation did that, St. Gabriel's would become a living manifestation of the Vine, Christ in the world. It must be possible—it worked for us, and we're nothing special.'

'Is it as simple as that, though?' Ann argued. 'There are so many reasons why people could hold back from knowing Christ: pride, fear of the unknown, perhaps being unwilling to be different. Even more reasons for not allowing Him to be Lord in more than name!'

'That's exactly the point,' countered Tom. 'The Church today is nearly turning itself inside out to prove it is no different from the rest of the world. If we are in Christ we *are* different, gloriously different!'

'Outsiders might not see so much of the glory.' Ann seemed so sad.

Tom tried to encourage her. 'Just look at the way our relationship has changed, how much closer we are on a level that matters. Imagine how the atmosphere in church would be if everyone really loved one another. Ann, it would be fantastic! Think what the world would see then! No, we must certainly stand by St. Gabriel's, get to know people much, much better and share our new life with them.'

Now Ann had grasped the vision in her own terms. 'Of course! We hardly know anyone in the congregation; we never invite them for meals—how can we communicate with them at all?'

There was obviously a lot of work in all this, and they were suddenly overcome with tiredness. As they prayed together, they saw clearly that they could not barge in and take over the church—Christopher Dean would be the next person to contact. Yet the situation here was rather sticky: the last time they had seen him he had broken down in front of them. On the other hand they had been praying for him, and they knew enough now to expect results. It was a comforting thought on which to end the day.

'Of course! Tony!' With eight hours' sleep and a morning cup of tea behind her, Ann was suddenly in control of the situation once more.

'What do you mean?' asked Tom.

'We could telephone Christopher Dean to let him know that Tony is coming out of hospital.' Tom was uncertain as to the wisdom of this, but Ann persisted.

'We don't want him to go looking for him at the hospital and not be able to find him. And he'll think us very rude if we don't tell him, especially after the trouble he took in seeing us the other morning.'

'He's probably still feeling embarrassed about that,' suggested Tom. Rather reluctantly he agreed that Ann should telephone. The result was disappointing. Dean greeted the news with polite enthusiasm, said nothing about their previous conversation, and ended the call abruptly by hoping that Tony would be well enough to enable them to bring him to church on the following Sunday. Ann could not hide her disappointment.

However, St. Gabriel's did seem different to Ann when the family occupied their usual pew for parish communion. Everybody appeared as remote as always, but she could enter into the worship with joy, for she knew Jesus to be truly present. On more than one occasion, Angela looked at her mother with concern because she was singing louder than usual. The act of receiving the bread and wine was particularly precious. Again, she was conscious of her face burning, and the desire to open her arms to greet her Lord.

The only thing that marred their morning was that Christopher obviously didn't share their joy. If anything, he seemed more serious and withdrawn than usual. That was understandable if he was going through the kind of conflict that they had experienced. His sermon was brief and to the point, the message clear: don't commit yourself to anything unless you intend to see it through. As they left at the end of the service, he was as polite as ever and thoughtful enough to avoid giving Tony the usual pat on the head. He made no reference to the subject that was uppermost in their minds.

For weeks they maintained their prayer for their rector, humbly asking the Father to draw His servant into a deep awareness of His love for him. Ann was moved to pray in her strange tongue. The Holy Spirit who inspired this prayer within her, she felt, knew better than she how to pray for Dean. She became increasingly frustrated at being unable to do anything to help the situation. 'Keep praying,' Tom told her. 'God can do more about it than you can.' She didn't question this truth, yet it would still have been good to have something to do. Whenever she prayed, the words 'Abide in me' kept filling her mind. Years of senseless activity had to give way to a dependence upon God, and she was not finding the transition easy.

Then, one evening, they were surprised by an unannounced visit from Christopher. He seemed a little embarrassed when Tom showed him into the lounge. He refused the offer of tea or coffee, and they chatted aimlessly for some minutes. After a natural lull in the conversation, he finally came to the reason of his visit.

'I believe we have a mutual friend,' he said, keeping his eyes fixed on the pattern of the carpet. 'During the past weeks I have had several conversations with Alan which have been both enlightening and challenging.' He paused, uncertain as to how to continue. 'I realise that I have come to a crucial point in my life and ministry, and that I have a series of very important decisions to make. One of these involves you closely, I believe. Before I tell you more of that, there are a number of questions I would like to ask you.'

For over twenty minutes, he questioned both Tom and Ann about their meetings with Alan, the changes that had taken place in their personal lives, and Tony's remarkable healing.

'I must confess that I had thought the days of miracles were over. I have always taught that they were an initial evidence of God's anointing upon the Church, and that we shouldn't look for such signs now. However, in this case it looks as though it must be attributed to some intervention on God's part. That is not an easy admission to make . . .' His voice tailed off and he sat silently for some moments, lost in his own thoughts. Tom finally interrupted.

'How does one of your decisions affect us?'

'Oh, I am sorry. I have such a lot on my mind at present.' Again he paused, uncertain how much he could confide in them. 'I want you to give me your assurance that this conversation will remain strictly confidential. It isn't usual for a parish priest to discuss such things as this with his parishioners.'

Tom and Ann wondered what was coming next. Both readily agreed to the request.

'Alan has shown me that I have never truly placed my life in God's hands. That has come as quite a shock; I have been in the ministry for over twenty years. Even in that time I have not given the control of my life over to Christ, but, if anything, have tried to manipulate Him into my way of thinking. You have yourselves tasted some of the results of my bitter failure over these past years. I have often seen people's needs and desired to meet them, but have been powerless to do so. I know that I need to pass over my life and ministry into God's hands and ask for that empowering of His Spirit which I believe you have both received, though in very different ways. That is one decision I have to make.

'Another affects the life of St. Gabriel's. Alan has pointed out to me that there seems little point in my seeking personal renewal in my life unless I am prepared to lead the people of St. Gabriel's into a similar renewal of their lives.'

Tom and Ann exchanged glances. God was answering more than one prayer at the same time. The rector continued, 'I confess to you that this fills me with considerable fear. We have always been a very conservative congregation with a considerable tradition behind us. I hate the thought of upsetting any of our faithful worshippers. That this would be inevitable I realise from my own turmoil during recent weeks, and I am sure you have experienced a similar time of disquiet in both your lives. Frankly, I don't know how many members of St. Gabriel's would want anything to do with this sort of thing. They're all busy people with lives of their own to lead and they might well resent any move on my part to suggest that their spiritual lives are inadequate and fall short of God's plan for them. I suppose I am uncertain as to how many really care about God's purposes. But Alan has made me face the fact that there is no place for me in the ministry unless I am faithful to the One who called me.'

He looked very sad. Tom and Ann wanted to reach out to him with words of reassurance, but they would only be an intrusion. They waited for him to continue.

'The task is quite awesome. I can only undertake my part in it if I can be certain of your assistance; I would need your support and encouragement. The alternative I do not

85

like to consider. I could resign, but I don't believe that is what God wants. If I go on, it must be because I am prepared to face up to the implications of living my life for the glory of God and leading others to do the same.'

Tom and Ann admired his honesty; it must have been difficult for him to come and say such things to them. Tom spoke for them both.

'Rector, you can be sure of our unqualified support should you decide to go ahead. None of us can know what that means. We are in this together and with God's help we shall see the whole of St. Gabriel's come to life.'

The priest smiled. That was a dream he had often had. He had hoped that one day it would simply happen, without making any demands upon him. If only he was ten years younger! He shrank from the prospect of a major upheaval.

'Thank you, Tom. I thought you would say that, but I had to hear it for myself.'

'And does it make any difference?'

'Yes, it makes a difference. It means that I have one less excuse for not doing what I know I must do.'

'You sound as if you are only prepared to enter God's kingdom kicking and screaming.' Ann's voice seemed strident after the mellow tones of the men. Christopher Dean looked at her. She held his gaze.

'My dear Ann, thank you for that. Perhaps that was why I needed to come this evening, to hear that. Here I am feeling sorry for myself, lamenting the task appointed for me, and all the time God is wanting to lead me into His kingdom. Would you both please pray with me?'

Neither moved.

'You mean . . .' Tom didn't know how to finish.

'I mean that I have come to the end of the line I have been travelling on. Tonight I am switching tracks. You said we were in this together. I take that to mean we are travelling in the same train, our coaches joined to one another. That co-operation we are going to need had better start now. I want you to ask God to baptise me in the Holy Spirit. I have been reading some books about this; I believe it is usual to lay your hands on a person's head when you pray with them.'

Ann wanted to insist that nobody had ministered to them personally in this way, but the rector fell on to his knees in the middle of their lounge carpet. To refuse his request would seem most ungracious.

'Lord, in these last days I have confessed to you all my past failure and disobedience. I can only submit myself to you now and ask you to make something out of the wreck of my ministry. You know how afraid I am of what the future may involve. I can only give you these fears now and ask you to give me all the confidence that I am going to need to remain faithful to you. I ask you to baptise me with your Holy Spirit and to renew your church at St. Gabriel's. And I thank you for Tom and Ann; I am most grateful that I do not have to face the future alone. Amen.'

Tom and Ann felt humbled by hearing another man's prayer to God. They placed their hands on the rector's head. 'Lord Jesus,' Tom began haltingly, 'we thank you for Christopher and we thank you that you have brought him to this moment before you. Thank you for answering our prayers. Please baptise him now with your Holy Spirit. Fill him, Lord, with your Spirit of love, joy and peace and give to him the boldness he needs to lead your people here in the way that you choose.' Having joined in the 'Amen', Ann began to pray out loud in the unknown tongue that God had given her. While both she and Tom were speaking, they were conscious that the rector was breathing deeply, his hands open in welcome to the Lord. When she had finished speaking in tongues, Tom again spoke, knowing the words came not from his mind, but from the Spirit of God.

'My dear son, for many years I have waited for this moment. Now the dry water-course shall be filled with water. It shall flow as a torrent to bring life to the parched grazing lands where my sheep languish. Rejoice and be glad in the promise that I make to you now. As I have always remained faithful to you, so shall you remain faithful to me. You have been until now a sapling blown easily in any direction by the wind. I shall make of you a sturdy oak that shall withstand the battering of many storms.'

In the silence that followed, each gave thanks to God. Then Christopher began to sing 'O worship the King, all glorious above.' The others joined in lustily, heedless of the sleeping children upstairs. Christopher had risen to his feet during the singing, and they ended the verse embracing one another like long-lost friends. He left them rejoicing, thankful that he had not brought his car. He felt intoxicated. Then he remembered that the inhabitants of Jerusalem took Jesus's disciples to be drunk when they were filled with the Holy Spirit on the Day of Pentecost. No wonder, if they felt anything like himself.

8

THE FOLLOWING DAY was Sunday. Christopher Dean cele-
brated holy communion apparently lost in rapture. Ann
was amused at the stifled comments of some of the congregation. It was as if he had been released from something
that had restricted him for years. Now he was free to enjoy
what he was doing. He preached on the first of the beati-
tudes: 'Blessed are the poor in spirit, for theirs is the kingdom of heaven.' He was obviously being careful not to
allow his enthusiasm to run away with him; he would have
caused misunderstanding and consternation if he had told
of the events of the previous evening. Instead he spoke
with a new conviction and note of authority, without losing
any of his graciousness or gentleness.

He greeted Tom and Ann with a broad grin at the end
of the service and asked them to wait until everybody else
had dutifully filed out.

'I wanted to thank you,' he said. 'I might have known I
couldn't have gone on resisting if you had been praying for
me.' His eyes twinkled.

'There is nothing to thank us for,' said Tom. 'Just thank
God as we are doing. The fruit is already evident in you.'

'Really?' said the rector, genuinely surprised. 'I've had a
wonderful time; never enjoyed worship so much! Even

preaching was a thrill, and I've always found it most demanding and difficult. It isn't only for last night that I want to thank you, but for the last few weeks.'

'What have we done in that time, except pray for you?' asked Ann.

'You said nothing, Ann. That was very important. You could have said all kinds of things that would have put pressure on me and might well have made me react differently. The evening you phoned me with news of Tony I was afraid you were going to, and I cut you off rather abruptly. I'm sorry for that.' Ann and he smiled at each other. 'I'm also thankful you didn't go running round to other members of the congregation with this Holy Spirit business. I've heard of that having devastating results in some churches. Now we can prayerfully consider together how God wants us to proceed from here; I'm finished with working in my own strength.' Brave words! thought Tom.

The three of them decided to meet on the following Tuesday to pray together.

'Perhaps your wife would like to come, Rector,' suggested Ann. He looked embarrassed.

'Er, I don't think she is quite ready yet, Ann. And by the way, I hope my fellow branches aren't going to carry on calling me rector!'

Ann smiled. 'Anything you say—Christopher.'

Their meeting turned out to be extremely valuable. It was to become the first of many such meetings, and laid the foundations for future thought and discussion. Alan's teaching to Christopher about the Church began the conversation, and however far they followed their own thoughts they usually reached the same conclusion as he had outlined. Apparently Alan felt he should let them explore by themselves now, for having set the scene he had ɔowed out. Yet his teaching and his faith remained central to future developments, and he was always at the end of a telephone if needed.

Tom and Ann felt they already knew quite enough theory about the Church, but apparently Alan had discussed it from rather a different angle with Christopher, and they were interested to hear what Christopher had to report.

'The concept of submitting your will to the Lord's and living for His glory is quite difficult to adapt to until you realise He knows best,' began Christopher. 'Then you have to cope with submission to other members of the church, accepting your position without pride, jealousy or anger. I need to learn a lot more about that.'

'Surely repentance and continued submission to God are the keystone of your relationship to others,' suggested Tom. 'Without this, your spiritual life as an individual or as a church is crippled and eventually destroyed.'

'The opposite of submission must be rebellion, I suppose,' Ann contributed. 'Call it disobedience if you like, but it was serious enough for God to throw Satan out of heaven, and it also caused sin to come into the world. Isn't it reassuring to see a principle which applies so constantly, from Adam in the Garden of Eden to me trying to impress myself with my own efficiency? Rather daunting as well, though.'

'You can say that again.' Christopher made a wry face. 'I was nearly completely broken when I saw my disobedience in its true perspective. I thought I had been serving God all these years, running His business quite well for Him. When I realised how I had been working outside His will, even against it, and leading others to do the same, my life became something I was deeply ashamed of. Despite that, I realised people still looked to me for leadership—and what a responsibility that is! Unless they see submission to God in my life, I can preach repentance at them until their Sunday dinners grow mould, and they won't see the point. This was what was weighing me down when I came round last Saturday and asked you to pray for me. It is only in God's strength that I can face the future now.'

'Whereas we, your "sheep", need to see that an hour and a half in church on Sunday is a pitiful sort of obedience to God,' countered Tom. 'And that has some hefty implications as well. The way we use our time, money, house, character, energy—everything needs reviewing, and Ann and I have hardly begun to consider the implications yet.'

'I wonder how the rest of the church can be made to see these truths,' said Ann, broadening the scope of their conversation. 'I can see most of them running a mile.'

'That's another thing I've been thinking about.' The rector looked grave. 'I've always measured my success in terms of numbers in church; but what sort of a priority is that? Nobody has ever asked me about the spiritual depth of my congregation. If some people are utterly opposed to what I try to do, given of course that we proceed with utmost caution and deference to their feelings, I cannot let them deflect me from God's will. This is going to require a great deal of prayer, but it is obvious we cannot be faithful to God and popular with everyone.'

'Have we managed to be either, so far?' Ann's question was rather near the knuckle, but Christopher had to concede that they had probably failed on both fronts.

'I'm quite overwhelmed by all we have to do,' said Ann honestly.

'Just a minute, though, Ann,' Tom broke in. 'What do

you think we have to do? Surely God has promised He will do it. Let's not get back into a whirlwind of activity like before, without doing it in God's strength.'

'We are sent out in the Spirit's power to do His will,' added Christopher, 'like messengers. In fact, I was thinking about angels today, and God taught me a lot about them. They are His messengers, and yet most of their time is spent simply praising Him. They are content to wait upon Him and only leave His presence to do a specific job when He sends them. They go in the knowledge that they will succeed, because they have been sent with His power and authority.' There was silence as these ideas were appreciated. 'The wonder is,' he added, 'that often God has to be so patient with us and still seems to bless our activity. Imagine a father watching a child struggle with something. There is a very simple solution to the problem, but the child refuses all offers of advice or help. It isn't until the child recognises that he will never succeed by himself that the father can intervene.'

'You never used to explain things so clearly,' commented Ann, causing him to blush slightly.

'Once we've seen that,' he continued, 'the big danger to avoid is saying "Jesus lives in me, so whatever I do, I can be sure of success through His power." Such an attitude will only result in us falling flat on our spiritual faces.'

'Goodness,' said Ann, 'doesn't all this run contrary to the way we have lived until now?'

'Yes, indeed,' exclaimed Tom. 'We have all been brought up to be independent. "Stand on your own two feet and never let anyone wipe your nose for you," I was always told.'

They laughed at his impersonation. It diverted their attention only momentarily.

'It's going to mean a great change in our church life if we apply all we have discovered tonight,' said Ann. Christopher agreed.

'We seem to have a lot of theory,' Tom added, 'but I'm sure, as you say, that God now wants us to get on with the application of it.'

'Empowered by His Spirit,' Ann reminded him.

'I think it's time we prayed,' suggested Christopher.

During the following weeks, the three of them met regularly to talk and pray. A deep bond was being created between them. God, it seemed, had taken hold of their three lives to lead them in a new direction together. None realised how much this unity had come to mean until they were separated during their annual holidays. Christopher and Molly went to Scotland; Tom and Ann took the children to Wales.

The Billings had always enjoyed this time when they could devote themselves to each other and the children. They seemed to discover that they were more human once they were thrown out of their unthinking daily routine. This year they could also discover more about the Bible and prayer, and see the changes that had come about since God had become real to them.

Tom was struck by the joy Ann radiated. Her mouth only stopped smiling to sing. Sometimes he experienced jealousy—Ann seemed to be constantly filled with a vision of Christ, which was only granted him after struggle in prayer, and which then faded fast.

Ann in her turn was impressed by Tom's constancy and determination to conquer those aspects of his life which he knew offended God. He didn't always succeed immediately, but that just made the victory more meaningful when it came. Often they were only small things, but this was adding up in both of them to an increasingly clear demonstration of the power of the Spirit.

When they returned refreshed from their holiday there was a letter on the doorstep from Christopher who would not be back for another week. His holiday was obviously quite different from theirs.

Molly is only disquieted when I try to explain my new life to her. She wants to remain a normal, sensible Christian and the wife of a rector who is admired and respected by his parishioners. She openly resents my meetings with you although she says they can only be a 'passing phase', and she shrinks from any mention of the Holy Spirit. It is not in my power to explain things to her—she must meet God for herself. I only pray that it will not need a shock like Tony's accident to bring her to the Lord. Neither do I have the option of turning back on my decision; I may lose my reputation as a steady traditionalist, but there is no point in being honoured by men at the expense of disobedience to God.

I spend a great deal of time in Bible study and prayer. I cannot begin to tell you all I am learning from John 15. May I just summarise a few points without noting my reaction to them, since I know you share in my joy?

I need to make time to enjoy Christ. Must absorb what He is saying. Fellowship in the Vine should leave no room for loneliness (but think of Miss Higgs and Mrs. Trace). We must depend on the other branches and not think of ourselves as indispensable—we can all learn from each other (N.B. Rector!).

Renewal of church not our burden (Hooray! Hallelujah, I mean.) Work of God's Spirit, if we make our lives available to Him for that purpose. 'Apart from me you can do nothing.' i.e. nothing that is fruitful, nothing that He values. Must stop rushing around in a blaze of self-activity—repentance means more to Him. Should not do anything, in fact, unless we can do it in Christ. If we do it in Christ we shall see Him working in ways we thought impossible. 'With God all things are possible.'

Life without Jesus is without purpose. Man is left to his own inspiration and resources. (Had enough of that kind of living.) God will supply all power necessary to do His purpose: because of His great love He doesn't want us to fail. But also in love He will allow us to fail when we depend on ourselves.

We must also depend on other members of the body in relationships of genuine love—we should be able to depend only because we are committed to one another. (Don't look too closely at St. Gabriel's!) Should look for opportunities to serve them, and also be prepared to accept love and kindness from them—more difficult.

Need to see things as God sees them. 'We have the mind of Christ.' Fascinating. We can face anything in confidence because we are in Christ.

God desires to see the fruit of answered prayer in our lives. Prayer is not trying to persuade Him to do something He doesn't want to. Ask in confidence and faith. Confidence comes from abiding in Christ. Spirit will guide our prayer to ask what is right—use gift of tongues.

I could have written these things many times, considered many aspects, but that will have to wait until we can meet. You appreciate most of this is theory which I have not yet worked out in practice. I hold you before the Lord every day, and know you are doing the same for me. Look forward greatly to our next meeting—blessing be on you,

Christopher

As they read it through, Tom and Ann recognised many thoughts they had discussed together before, but they knew too the wonder of coming back to the same basic truths in different contexts. It was taking some time to adjust to the reversal of the values they had held for so long.

Christopher visited them a few days after his return and saw his letter on the table. They had meant to bring up one or two points, but Christopher had something else on his mind.

'All that is only one side of the coin.' He waved his hand at the pages with a dismissive gesture. 'More recently I've been trying to come to terms with the cost. It hurts, basically.'

'But think how small the material privations are compared with what you have gained,' Ann said trying to dispel the air of gloom in a tone of voice which, she realised too late, sounded smug. She was grateful that Christopher didn't pick her up on it. Why was it so difficult to express true faith without giving the impression you had all the answers?

'I'm not considering giving up any of our ideals, Ann, but we must calculate what we are letting ourselves in for, or the idealism may shatter when we crash back to reality.'

'Could we turn back?' The idea seemed quite new to Ann. 'I mean, do we have the choice?'

'There is always an alternative to following Christ,' Tom cut in, 'but I don't see that it could be worth taking.'

'The sacrifices will vary from one person to another; so each has a decision to make. What is increased fellowship to one is lack of privacy to another; a sense of purpose in Ann may appear a greater work-load to you, Tom. All I am suggesting is that we should weigh the pros and cons instead of kidding ourselves that it will be all joy and peace and no problems!'

For over an hour they continued their discussion before Christopher began to expound what he believed God had been telling him about the next step.

'Obviously, we need to teach others what we have learnt. This brings in problems of not bulldozing anyone into a decision, quelling spiritual inferiority complexes, and goodness knows what else. The job is vast, and yet I believe it has been entrusted to the three of us. Alan is far too heavily committed elsewhere to be any more than an occasional visitor.'

'I can't see me doing any teaching,' objected Ann. 'The very thought of standing up in front of an audience turns my knees to water. Surely you're better equipped for that.'

'I am trained to teach, certainly,' agreed Christopher, 'but in terms of the new way of life we are propounding, I have if anything rather less than you to offer in the way of experience. Anyway, I wasn't thinking of handing over my pulpit, exactly.' They smiled at the idea.

'What do you have in mind then? It sounds pretty concrete already.' Ann was enthusiastic, being more at home with practicalities.

'As I see it,' Christopher began cautiously, 'we would invite a few people round to the rectory and discuss things in a semi-formal atmosphere. I have been praying about this and believe that God has been suggesting some names to me. I know that sounds very cocksure, but they are so unexpected that in some cases they would never have occurred to me, which makes it more plausibly God's work.' He paused to allow the others to contemplate the idea. 'Any thoughts?'

There were several from both of them, but on the whole the idea appeared to meet the needs of the situation. Ann was all for it, with a continued reservation at the thought of doing anything too prominent herself, while Tom was concerned that there would be a great negative reaction.

'People won't object—they just need to be taught, surely.' Ann was almost gushing, and Tom felt guilty at his lack of enthusiasm. Prayer seemed a good idea.

They prayed through the situation from all angles: themselves, the people to be invited, the possible hindrances—it was a long time before they lapsed into silence. Ann had opened her eyes and nearly offered them more coffee when Tom suddenly spoke.

'My children, do not fear to follow the way that I set before you. You shall not walk alone, for I shall be with you to love, support and encourage you. Depend upon me and you shall share my joy in seeing the lives of many people change, and you shall rejoice in the healing that many shall receive. Do not walk with fear, but with boldness, for it is I, the Lord, who call you to lead my people to new life in me.'

Again there was silence until Tom opened his eyes and discovered the others looking intently at him. 'The words just came, like before.'

'Well, don't look so worried about it,' said Christopher. 'God has used your mouth to speak to us, to encourage us. There's no doubt about it; we simply can't turn back now, even if it costs us everything.'

9

TOM FELT RESTLESS that night: sleep eluded him. Countless times he turned over in bed, trying to still the turmoil of his thoughts, longing for the forgetfulness of sleep that would excuse him from facing the problem, at least for a few hours. But the situation was not to be evaded. Christopher's simple logic somehow annoyed him, although he had to confess the truth of what he had said. If God the Father Almighty told you to do something it was unthinkable to say 'No'. However, when you looked at all that was at stake, it wasn't easy to say 'Yes' either. Not that Tom was ungrateful. The Lord had supplied the missing dimension in his life. Now he was having to face the agony of realising that it was still his life. It was his home, his job, his family, his money, his life. He had given these to God; now it seemed that He was about to claim them as His own.

'Even if it cost us everything'—the words turned ceaselessly in his mind. What did they mean? The need for change at St. Gabriel's was obvious. Yet it seemed that they were going to need to face continuing changes if the life of their church was to be transformed in the way that seemed necessary.

Then there were those words of prophecy. So strange,

and yet so natural. The words were there and he felt only a sense of awe and peace once they were spoken.

The message that God seemed to be speaking to them was clear enough. 'Go on, don't stop.' It appeared that Ann was prepared to obey no matter the cost; she had fallen immediately into a deep sleep. That made the tension within him even more frustrating. Finally he decided to go downstairs and make a cup of tea.

Ann had left her Bible open on the kitchen table. She had been reading John 15 again. Tom glanced at the words, reading without thought. He stopped abruptly at verse 6: 'If a man does not abide in me, he is cast forth as a branch and withers, and the branches are gathered, thrown into the fire and burned.' A cold shiver ran down his spine.

Could it be possible? Having been part of the Vine and having tasted the riches of Jesus, could anyone really be 'cast forth'? Did God want that? Would he even allow it? The text seemed to give clear answers. What part would God have for him in Jesus, if he wasn't prepared to be fruitful?

He poured himself a glass of milk; he could not be bothered to make tea. He sat down on a stool and re-read the verse several times. 'If a man does not abide in me ...' He had been placed in the Vine by God's gracious act. He needed to go on living in Jesus, by obediently following the course that was set before him.

He felt tired. Tomorrow would be another very busy day at work, and he was tempted once again to try to lose himself in sleep. But something needed to be resolved first. He was quick to recognise that he wouldn't be able to abide in Jesus through his own self-effort or by displaying suitable works to gain merit marks; he would need to continue to live by God's free grace. This involved obedience. Would he dance to the Lord's tune, or not?

The consequences of not abiding seemed dire. 'He is cast forth as a branch and withers.' Only the Gardener Himself could perform such an act: He who accepted him in love! Tom caught something of the strength of God's love in this. It wasn't something weak or sloppy, but vigorous and strong. The work of the Vine was too important to carry a lot of dead wood, and he, Tom Billings, had no intention of being classified as that.

Tired as he was, he decided to spend some minutes in prayer before returning to bed. Soon he was at peace. Somewhere deep within his soul God seemed to be reassuring him. He was for God and for His way. He would trust that the Lord would lead him through the many changes that he would have to face in his life. He climbed the stairs feeling very tired, but much happier. The decision was made: only God's purpose for him mattered. The individualistic, self-assured Tom Billings was to submit to God and be obedient to Him. He slept soundly.

The same verse was having a very deep effect upon someone else that evening.

Molly Dean, Christopher's wife, had been infuriated throughout their holiday. Reading the Bible, scribbling notes and writing letters were activities that should be confined to her husband's study at home; such things were an intrusion on their time together. Not that she felt they were together. Christopher had changed recently. It was difficult for her to cope with the new depth of love he obviously had for her, and yet, at the same time, he had grown strangely remote and distant, absorbed in a new relationship that seemed to be more satisfactory than theirs. He claimed that this relationship was with God Himself. Certainly, she had never heard him talk about God in such free and intimate terms before, and this frightened her.

Christopher was the pillar of respectability, not only at St. Gabriel's, but also in the diocese. There had been several rumours that he could soon be offered promotion. 'A charming man; he should go far.' Throughout their married life she had grown accustomed to such comments and was now bitterly disappointed if anyone sagged in enthusiasm for her husband. This she regarded as a natural womanly pride in Christopher that was thoroughly healthy.

So it came as a shock when he began to view the life of St. Gabriel's in a new light. This mood of self-criticism did not suit him, or, at least, her image of him. He was saying things that could only be described as provocative, and she shuddered at the response that some of his comments, made to her in private, would evoke if they were made public.

On the positive side, the pensiveness that often used to enshroud him had apparently disappeared. She had grown accustomed to finding him sitting in his study in a thoughtful, withdrawn silence. Now he seemed to be filled with a new youthful enthusiasm and joy, so much so that there were times when she found him difficult to live with. She couldn't account for this change. Christopher had never been one for see-sawing emotions. He always gave the impression of being placid and in perfect control of himself. Molly had heard that it could be a bad sign for someone in a depressed mood suddenly to become elated, and she had waited expectantly for the return of the depression. Some weeks had now passed without any evidence to substantiate her fears.

It infuriated her to see Christopher's impatience for his meeting with Tom and Ann, and she had felt coldly indifferent towards him all day. She had done her best to keep out of his way, which, as there was plenty to do after their return from holiday, was not difficult. She worked hard, and by the end of the day she felt tired, the result of the tension within her as much as any physical exertion. At supper, Christopher rattled on about the new group that he was thinking of forming. She gently suggested another venue for the meeting, rather than the rectory, but the suggestion had not been received with any enthusiasm. The fact that he should jeopardise his career was bad enough; to do so in their own home was intolerable. She needed to think, and in her desire to be alone almost pushed him out of the house for his meeting with Tom and Ann. Then, ignoring the washing up, she gave her imagination free rein.

She pictured him coming to her tamely for forgiveness when this was all over, grateful for her love. Although he had made a fool of himself, she would still be prepared to love and respect him. Every man had a moment of folly in his life, and it was her duty to love Christopher through his.

On her lap lay a copy of the New Testament. She began to read the chapter in John about the Vine. All she had heard about for weeks was vines and fruit—or so it seemed. In fact Christopher had been strangely silent on the subject recently, but she suspected that this was in deference to her often-stated opinions.

The opening verses seemed strangely irrelevant. She couldn't imagine what all the fuss was about. She stopped short when she came to verse 6: 'If a man does not abide in me, he is cast forth as a branch and withers; and the branches are gathered, thrown into the fire and burned.'

Molly had always had a particular distaste for preaching about hell-fire and damnation. She considered it unnecessary to believe in the existence of the negative, and much more important to assert belief in the positive affirmation that God the Creator existed. As Creator He was entitled to be acknowledged by His creation and the job of the Church was to promote such acknowledgement. There was no need to try to engender fear in people to make them believe. That was sub-Christian, and she held strong views about the varying traditions of Christendom that had adopted such tactics to gain converts.

It never occurred to Molly that she or any who were prepared to acknowledge God would ever be rejected by Him. She considered herself a model of respectability, a virtuous woman who was a fitting example of the modern Christian, interested in the world's affairs without any pretence at being 'spiritual'.

Verse 6 angered her intensely; it was a clear word of rejection. Some branches were to be cut out of the Vine. That was totally inconsistent with her image of God. At once, she set about rationalising the text, which she found exceedingly difficult to do. It didn't seem adequate to suggest that Jesus was using thought-forms of His time, for there was no good reason why He should add this verse to the rest of the teaching concerning the Vine, unless He meant what He said. As to the burning, that she could not accept. To believe in hell would be to return to medieval terminology and thought-forms—a totally unthinkable thing to do. Yet, to her intense annoyance, she found that she couldn't dismiss what Jesus was saying. Could it really be true that some were going to be rejected, even some of those who had once been accepted by God?

Apparently, this was the sad lot of those who did not abide in Jesus. Molly thought hard about continuously living in Jesus. So those who didn't do this were to be slung out on their ears! No wonder her husband had always avoided talking to her about this verse; he would have been only too aware of her reaction!

Yet these words had begun a strange, unwanted line of thought in Molly. Was she accepted by God? Until that moment it had never occurred to her to doubt that. She had been a faithful church-goer since the sixth form at school, and surely her very position as rector's wife put the issue beyond any doubt. Then why this strange nagging doubt within her? Why the need to question the issue at all?

She slammed the book shut in annoyance and reached for a magazine. She flicked the pages over hastily, looking for something that would attract her attention sufficiently to take her mind off the question of acceptance and rejection. It was no use; her thoughts would settle on nothing else. With resignation, she turned to the New Testament again.

'I do live in Jesus. Of course I live in Him,' she told herself with confidence. Yet still the nagging doubt persisted. It was as if a voice within her was saying gently but persistently, 'Are you sure about that, Molly?'

'Stop crying!' Her mother's sharp voice echoed over the years of memory. 'It's not lady-like to be seen weeping.' It was years since she had surrendered to such a dreadful act: now she felt the need to cry. She just wanted to cry and cry; but no tears came. She sat there, feeling very angry and extremely sorry for herself. The truth was that she had never been accepted, not as a child anyway. She felt she could never satisfy her mother, and her father had seemed indifferent to her needs. She had not known what she could call genuine affection until she met Christopher. He seemed to understand her in a way her parents had never been able to do. He was gentle; he was considerate; he accepted her. He therefore was the acceptable man and it had become very important to her that everybody should accept him just as he had accepted her.

She realised that the reason for joining the Christian Union at school had been a childish belief that, if there was a God, He would surely accept her because she was part of His creation. It was preposterous for her to sit here, doubting this belief that had given her stability for so many years.

'We need to place our lives in the Father's hands,' Christopher had said. Such a suggestion made no sense to Molly. As far as she was concerned, her life was already in His hands. She found it beyond her comprehension that Christopher, a minister of many years' standing, should have found it necessary to do such a thing. How confused she felt! It seemed that the ground was being taken away from beneath her feet.

No, she was right. She couldn't possibly have been mistaken for all these years. Of course God accepted her. Then why did she never feel close to Him? Why was He always so remote and cold? Why could she not call Him 'Father'? The questions persisted one after another.

She was in turmoil. Her father had been indifferent to her; perhaps this heavenly Father was also indifferent. Perhaps He wanted nothing to do with her and had secretly resented her and laughed at her all these years. No, no. That could not be. If only she could cry! Instead, she flung the Testament across the room, knocking an ash-tray from the sideboard on to the floor with a splintering crash.

She sat stunned at her anger. She looked at the shattered glass lying on the floor, and saw her own life. Only a short while ago, she had been safe. Now she was feeling torn apart, dismembered, broken. Yet still she could not cry.

'God, help me.' The words formed themselves in the dark recesses of her mind. They needed to be spoken out loud; she knew they had to be spoken. But that would somehow be to submit to all the things she was fighting against. God was in His heaven to be acknowledged, not to be called upon to help stupid hysterical women like Molly Dean. She was so thankful that Christopher could not see her in this state. She must clear up the broken ash-tray before he returned home. She would not speak the words out loud. Her mouth seemed dry; her tongue stiff. 'I'm being stupid. I shall go to bed and forget the whole business.'

With great resolve, Molly cleared the broken pieces of glass from the floor, tidied the cushions on the sofa, turned out the lights and went upstairs. Christopher would be surprised that she had not waited up for him, but she could always make the excuse that she had a headache. She avoided looking at herself in the mirror as she removed her make-up—why, she was not quite certain.

It was apparent that, tired as she was, she was nowhere near to sleep. She picked up the novel which lay on the bedside table and began to read; still her mind could not be diverted from the conflict within her. She had not thought of herself as an angry person, but now she beat the pillows with her fists in sheer frustration. Then she lay back, panting with the effort, and stared up at the empty ceiling. Yes, it was quite empty. It contained nothing. There was a smudge here and there which indicated that the room was due for redecorating, but it did its job. It stayed up there, keeping out the elements, acting as a wall to guard the secrecy of their lives. This was their private room. This was her private life. Did it really matter if it was in God's hands, so long as the ceiling remained in position and didn't fall and crush her? That had been another childhood fear. It had seemed that there was nothing to support the ceiling as she lay in her bed night after night, burying the disappointment she had been to her mother. Occasionally, it was a pleasant thought that if it did fall it would end all her problems; then she would break out in a cold sweat, lest just that should happen.

It was years since that fear had engulfed her, yet even now she felt that familiar clamminess of her hands. She closed her eyes. Instead of an empty whiteness, there was now an empty blackness. That was even more lonely, even more fearful. Mother's voice sounded again, the threatening voice that had effectively been silenced in a host of buried memories. Why, oh why, should all these things come flooding back tonight? All because of that verse. Then she remembered that, although she had cleared away the broken glass, she had forgotten to pick up the Testament from where it had landed. It could lie where it was, if this was the kind of reaction it was going to invoke in her. Yet if she went downstairs and picked it up she would get out of this black and white emptiness for a while.

She opened her eyes. The ceiling was still there, looking blankly down at her. She was on the point of getting out of bed, when she heard the front door open.

'Molly?' It was Christopher. She was covered with confusion. What was she to say to him? Nothing; nothing, of course. These thoughts were private to her.

'Hello, darling. Sorry I'm a little late. Have you had a good evening?'

'It's been fairly quiet.' She knew she had failed to hide the strain in her voice.

'Are you feeling all right?' he asked with concern. He sat on the bed and took hold of her hand. 'You're in a cold sweat.' She pulled her hand quickly out of his grasp.

'I'm fine. Just tired. It's been a busy day. Do you want me to leave the light on while you undress?'

Christopher knew Molly well enough to treat these words in the way they were intended. 'No; I won't be a minute.'

'Good meeting with Tom and Ann?' She forced the polite question in an attempt to divert attention away from herself.

'Yes, thanks. We learned quite a lot.' Christopher noted that Molly made no effort to discover what they had learned. He climbed into bed and turned out the light. She turned her back on him with unaccustomed abruptness.

'Goodnight,' she said, coaxing as much sleepiness into her voice as she could manage.

That night Molly dreamed. In a cot a baby cried and cried. There was some satisfaction in the crying; it gave vent to anger. But there was emptiness too. Even in the crying there was emptiness.

10

CLAUDE WINTER BELIEVED in democracy. What is more, he believed that the Church should be administered on a democratic basis. Every member should have the right to determine the pattern of life of that particular congregation. He had always thought highly of Christopher Dean, because he was a rector who listened patiently and respectfully to his views, and had not made any decisions affecting the life of St. Gabriel's without due regard to Claude's opinions. Recently, however, Dean seemed to have changed and was no longer so eager for his counsel.

Hearing second-hand of the 'secret' meeting that was to be held at the rectory was the last straw. It was an unprecedented step to call a meeting to which he was not invited and of which he had deliberately been kept ignorant. One thing was certain. Such absurdity must be nipped in the bud. A personal confrontation was called for, and on his way to the rectory Claude Winter framed the wording of the letter he would write to the Bishop if their meeting did not reach a satisfactory conclusion.

What he could not know was that, for the first time in his life, Christopher was not afraid of Claude Winter and cared little for his opinions. The new sense of liberation he was now experiencing included freedom from the fear of being unpopular. Particularly, he was glad to be free from the tactics of those like Claude, who, he felt, considered it their God-given right to oppose everything in the name of democracy, and did their utmost to prevent any development that did not conform to their personal wishes.

Christopher had a new vision of such people. It seemed they didn't desire to contribute to the life of the church, only to prevent others from doing so, or complaining bitterly when they didn't. Were these fruitless branches? If so, they stood in danger of a dreadful judgment because they were also preventing others from becoming fruitful.

This aroused a new concern. That Claude should not be part of the first group was absolutely clear in his mind. In that gathering there needed to be those who would be open to the Word and Spirit. Yet Claude was important, as every member of St. Gabriel's was important. Christopher felt a great desire to break through the man's self-opinionated pride to bring him to a point of genuine repentance before God.

The meeting of the two men would be stormy, and Christopher sensed that this was a testing time. He must not on any account back down from the truth. It was not a question of his opinion as opposed to Claude's views. It was the revelation that God Himself had clearly given to Ann, Tom and himself against the blustering of a well-meaning but spiritually blind man, who none the less needed to be loved.

Christopher braced himself as he heard Molly answer the door-bell and greet Winter in the hall.

'Evening, Dean.' His manner was deliberately brusque and he carefully avoided the usual courtesy of 'Rector'.

'Hello, Claude; come in and sit down.' He still felt calm and peaceful.

'I'll come straight to the point.' He always did! 'What's all this "secret service" stuff? This is our church, you know. You've been acting strangely recently, as if you've got something going on that I don't know about. I'm being open with you; such things cannot go on. I'll resign from the Church Council unless I'm informed fully what all this stuff and nonsense is about—and I shall make a point of writing to the Bishop personally to tell him my reasons for doing so. You know my views. The church is a democracy. That means that I have a right to say what happens at St. Gabriel's and I have every intention of exercising that right.'

Christopher had a job not to smile openly at Claude's stupidity and pomposity. He recognised that such a flow of invective would have produced a very different reaction in him only a few weeks before. Claude Winter knew that, and was anticipating a sweeping and conclusive victory in one blast. He was surprised by the evenness and calm of Christopher's reply.

'I take it that you are referring to the meeting that is to take place here on the Thursday of next week?'

'So you do admit to calling a secret meeting?' challenged Winter.

'I have no desire to conceal it,' answered Christopher.

'But I haven't been informed about any meeting,' blustered the other.

'That is only because you haven't been invited.' Christopher was being as gentle as he knew how, yet now there was genuine rage in Claude's eyes.

'Haven't been invited! What the devil do you mean? I am a member of this church, I am a member of the council of this church. I have the right to be invited!'

'Do you want to come so badly?'

'I don't even know what the meeting is about.' Winter sprayed the carpet with spittle as he spoke.

'I believe God is wanting me to gather together a small group of people to share with them some of the wonderful things He has been doing in my life recently.'

Claude looked at him in stupefied silence for a moment. He had not expected God to be brought into the conversation.

'God doesn't want you to obliterate the democratic structure of the church. I have not approved any such meeting, and so I cannot be party to it. Neither will you,' he added pointing a finger accusingly at Christopher. 'You're not the first priest I've had to put in his place. You seem to think that because you wear that collar you are God Himself. Well, He gave me a mind and will of my own and I tell you clearly, Dean, that if you go on with this nonsense I shall do my best to break you.'

Could it really be that the placid life of St. Gabriel's during the past few years had hidden such attitudes, such anger, such misunderstanding, such pride? It came as quite a shock to Christopher that this was so. The time of reckoning was long overdue, but these were not the right circumstances for it to begin. Christopher had prayed for wisdom in dealing with Claude, and he silently and briefly reminded the Lord of his need for this now.

'Claude, it is difficult for me to understand why you should become so heated because I decided to invite a few friends to my home one evening.'

'You haven't invited me!'

'Surely, when you ask friends around for the evening you don't invite them all on the same occasion.'

'Do, if I'm having a party!'

'This isn't a party.'

'No? From what I gather quite a few are coming.'

'I can assure you that it will be very different from a party.'

'What's the purpose of it then?'

'To talk, mainly.'

'What about?' The questions were snapped out with military precision.

'I'm not too sure of the content yet, to be honest.'

Claude looked at him with suspicion. 'I've never known you to lie before.'

Christopher felt the anger rise within him. This was the danger point. 'I'm not lying, Claude. I honestly do not know what I shall say to that group; I am expecting God to make that clear to me in due course.'

'What's all this God business? I've always taken you to be a man with his feet firmly on the ground, who understood the ways of the world. Suddenly you sound as if you have received some great revelation from the Almighty.'

'You could say that.'

Claude looked at him now with disbelief. Suddenly he seemed to calm down and he leant forward in his chair.

'I say, Christopher old chap, you are feeling all right,

114

aren't you? I mean, nothing's wrong, is there? We've always been friends, haven't we? You can confide in me!' This time, Christopher did smile openly.

'Everything is fine, thank you, Claude. I'm not going mad; in fact things have never been better.'

Winter seemed perplexed as to how to continue. Now that his mood had changed, he somehow couldn't return to their conversation with the same venom. Christopher sensed his unease.

'Look, Claude, you have seen that I have changed. That is because God has changed me. I know that he wants to change all of us at St. Gabriel's so that we can know Him better and serve Him more faithfully.'

It was as if a bomb had exploded in the room.

'For fifteen years, I've served this church faithfully. Are you now suggesting that my service hasn't been good enough? That there are others who serve better? Well, are you?'

'I believe that none of us has properly understood what it is to serve the Lord, and I include myself in that.'

'I don't understand what has happened to you, Dean, but I don't like it. If that meeting goes on here next week, then I shall resign from the Church Council—and I shall see fit to withhold my financial support from St. Gabriel's.' Winter expected that to be decisive. The church's finances were never healthy and there had been more than one occasion when he had been lauded as the generous bene-factor who had saved the congregation from acute financial embarrassment. Christopher took the blow without flinching.

'I have no intention of cancelling that meeting, Claude. If you feel you must resign then I shall respect your decision.'

'So you want me out of it,' he challenged.

'No, Claude, I want you very much in it.'

'It doesn't sound like that.'

'Nevertheless, it is the truth. I simply need to be faithful to what I believe God is telling me to do. I'm sure that the time will come when I shall want to invite you to a similar meeting; but not this one.'

'I'm not arguing with you any more, Dean. You haven't heard the last of this,' he said as he opened the study door. 'Unless you change your attitude, you will suffer the consequences of your actions.' With that he slammed the front door and was gone.

Molly stood in the study doorway. Christopher only had to look at her face to know that she had heard Claude's raised voice. 'Well?' he asked inquiringly.

Molly said nothing. She turned away and returned to the kitchen. Christopher felt very alone.

Winter avoided his gaze on the Sunday, and Christopher's only moment of disquiet was to see him deeply engrossed in conversation with a group of like-minded people at the end of the morning service. There was much nodding of heads and he sensed a stir of rebellion within the fold.

For one day Christopher wavered. His church seemed about to split and his marriage was under greater pressure than ever before. He wanted to believe that God had everything under control, and yet it was the intrusion of God into his life that had brought about the present situation. He needed an objective view to help him out of this vicious circle, but didn't know who to turn to. Tom and Ann had prayed with him about it, but they, like himself, were too close to see clearly. After spending most of the day failing to prepare the content of the first meeting, and with depression closing in around him, a name dropped into the confusion.

116

'Alan!' He reached for the phone.

Alan couldn't come until nine, after another meeting, and it was a very suspicious, tight-lipped Molly who made them coffee. Sudden meetings late at night did not fit into her concept of Christopher's work. She was barely polite.

'How can I help her?' Christopher began as soon as she had left the room. 'She is suffering so much, and yet I can't get anywhere near her.'

'Perhaps you're not the best person to do anything direct,' answered Alan. 'It's very important that her faith should be in Christ, not in your faith.'

'Can I do nothing but pray, then? It's very difficult when she seems to become more bitter and cold every day.'

'If she is aware of conflict, then something is happening. You would have more to worry about if she wasn't moved in any way by the change in you.' Alan's voice was low and sympathetic.

'But why is it taking so long? Why can't she see?'

'I think you will find there is some block, some psychological reason why she cannot give in—because that is how she undoubtedly sees it, as a defeat. Perhaps you should pray that God will reveal that block to her, or to someone else, perhaps to yourself. It's not too easy to make such pronouncements when I hardly know her, but that's what I would do.'

'I didn't expect you to come up with miracle answers, Alan.' Christopher smiled. 'These are human matters and you can't solve them like an equation. Just having something specific to think and pray about is answer enough for the moment.'

'Shall we pray for a few moments now?' Christopher nodded gratefully, impressed by the understanding of this friend, and so glad he had remembered his offer of help from months ago. As they prayed there was no immediate revelation, no divine diagnosis spoken to them, but Christopher regained assurance in God, and peace returned.

'The other matter is even more pressing.' Christopher launched into the second problem, outlining Claude's demeanour, and the unease that was spreading throughout the church.

'God will not be able to work freely in you if you are paralysed by the first sign of dissension within the church,' was Alan's first comment, which seemed quite fair. 'People have to react in some way to the concept of a vital, living God. Claude has reacted adversely; the others' reactions are based on fear and misunderstanding. When they start seeing fruit in your life, the evidence may seem to point in a more positive direction to some of them.'

'I have been trying for several days to face the fact that a church cannot be renewed without conflict, any more than one individual can.' Christopher's face showed his anxiety. 'Christ's teaching caused many followers to leave Him, and if I preach the word of God faithfully, the same thing must happen here.'

'Would Claude be satisfied if you invited him to the meeting?' suggested Alan.

'I doubt it, really.' He paused. 'I think it would only give him more to gripe about. Anyway, that's not the point. There is a good chance that he would destroy any hope of new life in that initial group, and, under God, I cannot take that risk. If He wanted Claude there, He would have given me his name along with the others.'

'Have you thought about what you're going to say?'

'I've thought and prayed, of course, but it's a difficult matter. We are going to have to be honest with one another about the lack of reality in our individual spiritual lives and

118

in St. Gabriel's as a whole. That isn't going to be very comfortable.'

'Have you asked Molly to come?'

'I've invited her, but she wouldn't come near it. In her eyes I am ruining my reputation, my hopes of advancement, and under her own roof at that. No; she's not ready to face herself yet, above all not in public.'

'But Ann and Tom are coming.'

'Oh, yes. The time is not right for them to speak openly yet, but they need to be there to help me see where to go from here.'

Simply to talk with Alan had been a comfort and by the time he left at midnight Christopher felt greatly reassured. Before him was God's promise:'I will never leave you nor forsake you.'

There was an unusual air of expectancy in the room on the night of the meeting. All present had been in the rectory several times before; Christopher and Molly were well known for their hospitality. Yet none had been invited in circumstances such as these. Each had been interested in seeing who else was present and all were eager to discover the significance of the gathering. Tom and Ann were not usually seen at mid-week meetings at St. Gabriel's and had never spoken to some of the others present, although they had often seen them in church. Tom in particular felt the embarrassment of this in view of what he had learned in recent weeks.

As nobody seemed eager for conversation, Christopher began the proceedings punctually. 'Thank you all for coming this evening. I have something of great importance to share with you, something that will have a considerable bearing upon our life together at St. Gabriel's. I think it unlikely that I shall finish all that I want to say tonight, so I am going to ask you if you would be so kind as to agree to come back again next week and perhaps even the week after ...'

He had always been known for his brevity at meetings. It was intriguing to speculate on what he could have to say that would last two or three weeks!

I think it important that you don't go away tonight and decide not to return, because we are going to face up to several problems that we certainly cannot resolve in one evening.' His audience was attentive. 'I want you all to be honest with yourselves. It's so easy for us to close our eyes to certain truths because it is uncomfortable to face them. Now is the time for all of us at St. Gabriel's to face the truth about our relationship with God and how far our church life truly reflects what He is wanting of us. I have invited you here because I think each one of you will be prepared to face the truth.'

It was still difficult to gauge what people were thinking from their faces. He sensed the support that Tom and Ann were prayerfully giving him, even as he was speaking. Christopher decided that he should come directly to the heart of the problem.

'How many of you can honestly say that you know God, that you have a personal relationship with Him that is real and alive and meaningful?'

Nobody stirred. Tom and Ann instinctively felt that they should not direct attention to themselves at this point, so they too sat silently.

'I really want you to answer,' continued Christopher.

Mary Newell ventured a reply. 'Well, rector, I think most of us would admit to some kind of relationship with God, or we wouldn't be members of St. Gabriel's.' There was a general murmur of agreement.

'Are you doubting that we believe in God?' asked Stan Edwards, a local gardener, who was a much-loved character at the church.

'No, I don't doubt that, Stan,' replied Christopher. 'Nor do I doubt what Mary says. The question I asked, though, hasn't been answered. I didn't say "Do you believe in God?" or "Do you have any kind of relationship with God?" I said, "Do you have a relationship that is real and alive?" '

Again he was answered by silence.

'Have any of you experienced God speaking to you, for instance?' Christopher continued.

'I'm not in the habit of hearing voices, if that's what you mean!' Mrs. Baker's remark brought a ripple of laughter that broke the tension in the room.

'What are you trying to get at, rector?' Stan Edwards asked.

'I wonder whether we really understand what it means to be Christians,' he answered.

'Aren't you satisfied with us?' Miss Smith asked with a disbelieving frown.

'It isn't a question of whether I am satisfied or not, but of whether God is pleased.' The evening had not begun as Christopher had intended.

'How are we to know what God wants?' David Buckley was a quiet studious youth, in whom Christopher sensed there would be considerable spiritual depth.

'By having an intimate relationship with Him, so that we know His purpose for us. That is what I'm trying to ask. Do any of us have such a relationship?'

'We're not saints, you know.' Vanessa White was a young housewife, who had only been coming to St. Gabriel's for a few months.

'What are we then?' asked Christopher.

'We're just ordinary Christians, Mr. Dean,' answered Mrs. Baker, 'and very thankful that we are.'

Paul Rivers had been a churchwarden for three years. He was a mature man, whom Christopher greatly respected. The two had become close friends. Paul had noticed the change that had taken place recently in Christopher and had been worried about his reluctance to talk about his reasons for calling this meeting. Normally the two of them shared confidences about the affairs of St. Gabriel's naturally and easily. Paul, who had deliberately not entered the discussion so far, commanded considerable respect among the other members of the congregation and they were happy to sit back and allow him to be their spokesman.

'Christopher, I think you have something on your mind that you want to say to us. Why not go straight ahead and say it? I don't think any of us can see where all these questions are leading.' Paul's wisdom was always appreciated by Christopher and it crossed his mind that he might have been wrong not to have taken him into his confidence about the events of the past few weeks. However, it was too late to remedy that now. He was thankful that Paul had provided the right opening.

'Paul is right,' he went on. 'I have many very important things to say. To understand their significance will mean asking some basic questions of ourselves. You see, I have had to ask myself some very searching questions lately. I need to tell you some of the answers I've discovered.

'For many years I have been a parish priest and I have loved the job. It has been more like a way of life than a job, really. It has often been demanding, in some ways rewarding, but in many ways frustrating. I have grown to love the people I have tried to serve, yet increasingly in

122

recent years I have been weighed down by a sense of failure.'

The atmosphere in the room had changed. Christopher Dean, their much-loved rector, was not one to speak in such personal terms.

'There have been so many situations in which I have been unable to introduce people to God, to His love, to His healing power. The reason is a simple one. My own relationship with God was inadequate. I could not hear His voice, let alone be an instrument through which others would hear Him. As a result my faith and trust in Him were totally inadequate to face the responsibilities that are mine as a parish priest. You must all forgive me for the ways in which I have failed you. Even the way I have taught the people of this parish has fallen so far short of the Gospel, the good news of Jesus.'

Several would have liked to refute this self-critical analysis of his ministry, but no one spoke.

'In recent weeks, God has brought about a great many changes in my life. I am still grappling with the implications of these for the life of St. Gabriel's. I can already see clearly that each of us has been missing many of the riches that God wants to share with us. I have discovered that the Bible is full of wonderful promises that God makes to His people. Yet our ears have been deaf to them. We haven't even realised that He could do such things for us today.'

Christopher told briefly and simply how God wanted to give new life to His children. They had all been trying to serve Him in their own strength, loving God with their own resources. He pointed to the lives of Jesus's own disciples and how the Master had not allowed them to continue His minstry in the world after His resurrection until they had received the life and power of the Holy Spirit.

He went on to explain his realisation that a Christian was not someone trying to please God with his good deeds, but one who had been given new life by Jesus Christ, who lived that life in the power of the Holy Spirit and allowed God to produce in him the fruit that He desired to see.

His audience was deeply attentive to his every word. The flow of speech was interrupted only when Molly opened the door to announce that coffee was ready. Christopher was amazed to see that the time was approaching half-past nine. He had been speaking for well over an hour. What was even more surprising was that everybody had been listening so intently for so long.

He sensed that all, or nearly all, would return on the following Thursday. He would then introduce them to the Vine.

11

THE LETTER OF resignation duly arrived. Paul Rivers brought it by hand on the following Sàturday evening.

'I presume you can guess its contents,' he said as he handed the letter to Christopher.

'I have a fair idea,' he answered.

'The man is mortally offended.'

'Perhaps he needs to be, Paul.'

'I don't need to tell you that we are going to be hard hit

124

financially if he goes through with his threat to withdraw his support completely.' Christopher was pleased to see that Paul did not seem unduly concerned, judging by the tone of his voice.

'We can't run the church under continual threat, either,' said Christopher.

'Claude can make a great deal of unpleasant noise when he wants to.'

'I don't see how we can prevent him if that is what he's intent on doing. I don't relish the prospect; other people at St. Gabriel's won't know how to cope with it.'

'Then why not try to placate him—at least for a while.'

'How?'

'By inviting him to the next meeting on Thursday.'

'No!' Christopher was surprised by the emphatic tone of his voice. 'Listen, Paul. I don't understand any more than you what was happening last Thursday. All I know is that I spoke for over an hour and everyone sat there and heard me through, however surprised or confused they were by it. That's no credit to me; the words just spilled out of my mouth. I have thought about it a great deal since and it seems to me that the peace of God had somehow descended upon us. I know I was very conscious of the Lord's presence. Do you remember how Jesus appeared to the disciples after He had risen? He came into the room and said "Peace be with you." Well, it was something like that.'

'It was certainly different from any other meeting that we have ever had,' admitted Paul. 'What has this got to do with Claude?'

'Could you imagine him sitting quietly listening for over an hour? Why, after five minutes he would have been taking over the meeting, blustering away about his own opinions and trying to impress upon everybody their right of free speech.'

125

Paul had to laugh. He had stood by Christopher's side at countless meetings trying to control Claude's outbursts.

'God is going to do something important to change our lives at St. Gabriel's and I am sure that he doesn't want us to be distracted by worry about money. That will come with or without our friend Claude.'

'Do you want to see him leave St. Gabriel's?' Paul asked candidly.

'No, Paul, I don't want to see anyone leave. I desperately hope that Claude becomes part of the new St. Gabriel's; but he will have to change along with the rest of us.'

'You realise this talk of change is very threatening for most people?' Paul seemed very thoughtful.

'None of us likes change,' admitted Christopher. 'I've fought against it for years. I've fooled myself that God would be pleased and satisfied if we at St. Gabriel's were successful in perpetuating the good established traditions. I used every argument possible to satisfy myself. Yet deep down I knew it wasn't true. Every time I saw in the New Testament what the Church is supposed to be, I winced inside. We have hardly any conception so far of what it means to be the Church today.'

'Do you think the people will accept change?' asked Paul.

'They will have to—or leave.' The two men looked at one another. Both sensed that this was a great moment of truth for them, and indeed for St. Gabriel's.

'Like Claude?'

'Like Claude.'

'What happens if half the congregation leaves?'

'We have a congregation half the size, but one that desires to be faithful to God and be the kind of church that He wants.'

Paul sat thinking for several moments. The clock ticked loudly on the mantelshelf. 'Christopher, I've always respected you. Now you've changed, and for some reason I cannot easily define I respect you even more. I can't understand all that is happening at present, but I confess that the things you said last Thursday touched some very deep chords in my heart. For a long time, I have longed for more reality in my Christian life. It's funny; although we have known each other so long and have discussed freely together the affairs of the church, we never seemed to touch on spiritual matters.'

Christopher cringed at the truth of the statement but said nothing.

Paul continued, 'I agree with you; we are on the edge of something important. Frankly, I was hurt at first that you hadn't taken me into your confidence. Now I appreciate that you were right in not doing so. You had a great deal to absorb and learn. This process obviously took you some weeks and it wouldn't have been possible to give me a crash course personally.'

'Claude would not have appreciated that,' interrupted Christopher.

'No, you are right there.'

'You know, Paul, I think we have more important opposition than Mr. Winter.'

'Who?'

'You referred to them yourself.'

'Them?' Paul could not help appearing concerned.

'Yes. All those who will not want change. Those who will be simply apathetic. "I don't want to get involved," they will say. "I want things to carry on as I have always known them." They don't want their lives disrupted by anyone, even God. They are like suckers drawing life out of the church and giving nothing of themselves in return.'

Christopher had detected for himself the note of harshness that had crept into his voice. 'I'm sorry, Paul. "Judge not, and you will not be judged; condemn not, and you will not be condemned; forgive and you will be forgiven; give and it will be given to you; good measure, pressed down, shaken together, running over, will be put into your lap." ' Christopher closed the Bible which had lain open on his desk. 'I was reading those words just before you arrived. I am preaching on them in the morning. They are as truly for me as for anyone else. When we have learned the secret of giving, I think we shall then be very surprised at how much God has to give to us.'

They talked about the Vine. 'The apathetic ones will be like lifeless branches, you mean,' suggested Paul.

'I cannot see that there will be much fruit borne out of apathy or of being determined not to become involved in the whole life of the Vine,' replied Christopher.

Paul looked sombre. 'A fruitless branch is always a sad sight. Once it is cut off and begins to wither it looks pathetic. I was wondering whether a separated branch could ever be restored. Gathering and burning seem so final.'

'God is love,' answered Christopher. 'The Gardener is love. We can be sure that He knows every branch through and through. No gardener cuts away the whole branch at the first sign of unfruitfulness. He will nurture it in every way that he knows to bring it to the fruit-bearing stage. For him to remove the branch altogether is the last resort, which he reluctantly takes for the sake of the whole vine. For the one who continually resists God's nurturing...'

'I think we need to pray for St. Gabriel's,' said Paul, 'pray very hard.'

'Let's begin now,' suggested Christopher.

The two men had shared many conversations in recent years. This was the first time they had prayed together.

For Tom and Ann these continued to be days of revelation. They became almost overwhelmed by the nature of God's love, and this was having an effect on their daily lives. Selfish excesses were cut out; they ate well, but simply, and realised that security was no longer a good bank balance. Their weekly contribution to St. Gabriel's increased considerably, compensating for the loss of Claude's support. They also sponsored a child in the Far East, securing for him an education which he would not otherwise have had. In fact, they wanted to do much more, but Christopher assured them that their fellowship with himself and their prayer for St. Gabriel's were in themselves enough for the moment.

They had resigned themselves to this role when they were surprised by an unexpected visitor on the Saturday evening. Ann answered the door to find David Buckley, the young studious member of the group, outside.

'Good evening, Mrs. Billings. Please forgive me for calling on you like this, but I would like to talk to you and your husband.'

'Come in, please.' There was a note of genuine warmth in Ann's voice which didn't go unnoticed. 'It's David, isn't it?'

'Yes, that's right.'

'Well, I'm Ann and this is Tom.'

The two men shook hands. This was the first visitor that they had ever received from St. Gabriel's, except, of course, for Christopher.

David did not seem at ease, and his embarrassment forced him to launch straight into the reason for his visit.

129

'You didn't say very much at the meeting on Thursday, but I sensed that you already knew everything that Mr. Dean was going to say.' Tom nodded in agreement.

'I might tell you,' David continued, 'it was all rather a shock for me. You see, for about three months now I have felt that I should be ordained one day. I have already spoken to the rector about it. Now all my ideas of ministry seemed to be torn apart by that meeting.'

Ann frowned. 'I can't remember that we spoke about ministry.'

'We didn't,' countered David, 'but the implications of what was said would very clearly affect ministry. Even the rector admitted that he had felt frustrated and had failed the people of St. Gabriel's. That was pretty hard to take. I've always respected him and thought of him as an ideal parish priest. In fact, it is his example that has had a deep influence on my decision to seek ordination.'

'You have to be sure that God has called you before you take such a step, surely?' said Tom gently.

'Oh, I know, and I believe He has. However, I thought He was calling me to a safe occupation, a hard-working one mind you, but one built on the secure tradition of the Church built over many centuries. Yet when Mr. Dean was speaking, he went back even further to the tradition of the first disciples. And I realise now that the Christian life isn't the safe, quiet thing I thought it was. It's adventurous, exciting and fresh. Did you see Mr. Dean's eyes on Thursday night? They were sparkling. He's never looked like that before. And did you notice how everybody was engrossed in what he was saying? We were all caught up in the excitement with him, as he told us of the possibilities of a life filled with God's power.'

Ann couldn't help smiling. 'You're getting quite excited

about it yourself.' David too smiled, but couldn't help blushing at the same time.

'I'm not an excitable person, Mrs. Billings, I mean, Ann. I could picture myself as Mr. Dean was, a good parish priest. I cannot see myself as someone leading people into a close relationship with God, seeing them filled with the Holy Spirit and even being healed by the laying on of hands as Mr. Dean was suggesting.'

'That is only because you haven't experienced what Christopher has experienced in recent weeks,' said Tom.

'Or what you have experienced?' probed David.

'How do you know that?'

'It shows. I was across the room from you on Thursday. You were as engrossed as the rest of us in what was being said. We were all looking very serious because we were all engaging in a good deal of self-examination, even dear old Mrs. Baker. But you two were different. You were smiling. There seemed to be an inner contentment or peace about you. It was almost as if you were encouraging the rector, supporting him.'

Both Tom and Ann were surprised by these remarks. 'And then there was this,' said David as he drew a folded piece of paper from the inside pocket of his jacket. Tom recognised his own handwriting on it. He looked at David for an explanation.

'After you had left the meeting, I noticed this on the floor between the chairs where you had been sitting. That's why I asked the rector for your address, so that I could return it if it was important. I must confess I read it—just to see whether it *was* important, you understand.'

'And is it?' asked Tom.

'Yes. At least it has become important for me to understand what it means.'

131

'Read out what it says,' suggested Ann.

' "The Father rejoices in the Vine, in His Son, Jesus, and in everyone who lives in Him. For when the Father looks upon the branches of the Vine, He does not see them in isolation from Jesus; He sees them in Jesus. That means that the Father can only look at you and me "in Jesus". For we have no identity apart from Him." '

David now looked to Tom for an explanation. 'Look, David, I expect Christopher will be talking about all this next week, and he will probably make a much better job of it than I could. However, if you're not in a hurry, we could do a little Bible study together.'

At this point, Ann excused herself saying that she had to get the children's clothes ready for church in the morning. She left them with the promise of coffee when she had finished the chores.

As she moved about the house, the familiar patterns of tidying and ironing being automatic, she thought about the conflict that seemed to precede acknowledgement of God as a vital force—a conflict she sensed in David. She prayed intermittently, but persistently, for nearly an hour. As she started to make the coffee, Tom's voice called from the sitting-room.

'Won't be a minute; it's nearly ready,' she shouted back.

'Never mind the coffee; we have more important things to do; David wants us to pray with him to be filled with the Holy Spirit.'

The milk bottle she was holding slithered down on to a pile of spoons with a tremendous crash. Why was answered prayer such a surprise?

'I'm coming.'

On the following morning, David Buckley sat with Tom, Ann and the children in church. He was at peace. That inner restlessness had ceased and he was able to participate in the worship in a different way. The act of communion was a true meeting with Christ and he felt his face burning as he expressed his new-found praise quietly in tongues. It had surprised him when Tom and Ann prayed in tongues the previous evening. It surprised him even more to discover that his mouth was filled with strange syllables that somehow expressed the thoughts he could not formulate in English.

And it seemed that God Himself had given him a word of reassurance. 'Those who respond to my love know that I will never cast them off.' He felt that now he belonged to God and that he would always belong to Him. It was that knowledge that brought him such peace.

It was the lack of that knowledge that made the same act of worship a nightmare for Molly Dean.

12

'IF YOU ABIDE in me, and my words abide in you, ask whatever you will, and it shall be done for you.'

The words seemed to mock Molly. While Christopher had been deep in conversation with Paul Rivers in his study, she had spent Saturday evening with John, chapter 15. She was determined to find freedom, yet every attempt made her more desperate. The fact that her prayers did not seem to be answered only reinforced her belief that God had rejected her.

She felt as though she had lost her identity; then it became all too apparent to her that she had never had any true identity. Everything in her life had been a façade built to avoid facing up to her true self. She didn't have Christopher's new-found faith and assurance, and realised with horror that she resented him because of this, to the point of shunning physical contact. Yet in previous crises it was his love for her that had pulled her through.

Sunday worship was agony. The spoken words which seemed to claim and promise so much were empty of reality. The act of communion was false; she experienced no union with the Almighty, only an intensification of her own loneliness.

When Christopher had turned and said to the congregation, 'The peace of the Lord be always with you', it had taken great self-control to prevent herself from shouting back 'What peace?' Instead she had knelt down and buried her face in her hands and wept, trusting that to everyone else her actions would appear like an act of piety. In final desperation, she prayed a short simple prayer: 'Someone please help me.'

As soon as the service finished, she made for the door, only to find a hand on her arm. It was Ann.

'I'm sorry, Ann. I must hurry home this morning.'

'Molly . . .'

'Good-bye, Ann.'

With that she shook her arm free and with a few nods and smiles to other members of the congregation, she was soon out of the claustrophobic walls of the church building and into the sunlight. It was then that she realised that she had perhaps brushed aside the means of help she needed. She couldn't talk freely to Christopher at present; Ann was involved in this business and perhaps she would understand. She wanted to go back and apologise for her rudeness, but pride prevented her. She walked towards the rectory with the conflict increasing every moment.

She sat down at the kitchen table and sobbed. When the door-bell rang she was in no fit state to answer it and so she ignored it. Then to her alarm the back door opened and Ann walked into the kitchen. Molly tried to compose herself, but the effort was too great. She clung to Ann and cried and cried.

Ann had the wisdom to say nothing. She held Molly and was aware of a deep love for her, a love that was not her own.

Slowly, the sobbing ceased and Molly relaxed. She allowed herself to be held, feeling reassurance from the arms around her. It was fully five minutes before she gently released herself from Ann's arms.

'I'm sorry, Ann,' she said sadly.

'There's nothing to be sorry about.'

'Yes, there is. I was very rude to you in church just now.'

'You didn't intend to be.'

'No, I didn't intend to be. But then I keep feeling reactions that I don't want to feel and doing things that I don't want to do. Everything seems so hopeless at present.' She paused and looked enquiringly at Ann. 'What made you follow me here?'

'I don't know exactly. Towards the end of the service I felt that it was important for me to talk to you. I don't know why.'

'Perhaps this God of yours was telling you to,' answered Molly. Her voice could not disguise the tiredness she felt inside, nor the disillusionment.

'He's your God as well,' said Ann.

'Is He? Is He really? I thought He was until all this

business of knowing Him. I don't know Him—that's the problem. He won't be my God until I do.'

'Why should that be such a problem? Don't you want to know Him?'

'I didn't at first. I would have been quite happy for our lives to have continued as they were before. Christopher and I have had a good life together. Then he changed. I must admit that I now see many qualities that I hadn't noticed in him before. Still, the change has threatened our life together. He has changed and I haven't. I was resentful at first. I wanted him to be the way I had always known him. Our holiday made me aware of the futility of that wish. I realised that I would have to join him if we were truly to be together again.' Molly stopped. Why was she saying all this to a comparative stranger?

'And so . . .' prompted Ann.

'Oh, I don't suppose you're really interested in my problems. Let me make you a cup of tea.'

'No,' said Ann firmly. 'Making cups of tea won't help, will it?'

Molly sighed. She felt trapped. Dare she confide in anyone her true problem?

'You don't believe He wants you, do you?'

Molly looked up sharply. 'Who do you mean?'

Ann smiled. 'I mean God, not Christopher.'

'How do you know that? I haven't told anyone, not even my husband.'

'Let's call it feminine intuition,' suggested Ann.

'That's not intuition, and you know it,' challenged Molly.

'What does it matter? Is it true?'

'Yes, it's true.'

'Why do you think that?'

'I've tried this business of placing my life in God's hands

and nothing has happened. Absolutely nothing. In fact the very reverse. Any peace I ever had with God seems to have completely disappeared.'

Ann felt she was getting out of her depth. Christopher wouldn't be home for some time, as he was taking the Sunday School service. She shot a quick prayer heavenwards asking for inspiration.

'He does love you, Molly.'

'How do I know that? He has done nothing to prove His love to me. The only person who has ever done that is Christopher.'

'I love you, Molly.'

'Oh please, Ann. Don't give me platitudes. I can't stand any more.'

'No, I mean it. When I was holding you just now, I felt a deep love for you. I've never experienced anything quite like it before.'

'Part of this Holy Spirit business I suppose,' said Molly with some bitterness.

'I suppose so,' admitted Ann. 'There are so many changes going on in my life at present. It's difficult to keep up with them all.'

'The only changes that are going on in my life are for the worse,' said Molly tartly. 'I'm sure you came here to help me, Ann, and I'm grateful. But I don't think there is anything you can do for me.'

'I can pray for you.'

'Another platitude.'

'No, it isn't. Jesus says that if we abide in Him and His words abide in us we can ask whatever we will and it will be done for us.'

'John, chapter 15, I suppose.'

'That's right,' said Ann brightly, deliberately missing the sarcasm in Molly's voice.

'I've asked and He's done nothing for me. But I don't abide in Him, do I?' She threw the words out as a challenge.

'Molly! You're suffering from an overdose of self-pity.'

The two women faced each other in silence. 'I think you'd better go, Ann.'

Ann wanted to apologise for speaking the truth so bluntly, but no words would come. She picked up her handbag and opened the door. Was that really hate in Molly's eyes? She wanted to run to her, to hold her again and assure her of God's love for her. She sensed that the gesture wouldn't be received in the way intended.

'Good-bye, Molly.'

'Good-bye, Ann.'

She was almost in tears as she walked home. Had she failed the Lord?

Tom tried to reassure her by saying that she could have done no more.

'You don't understand, Tom. How would you feel if someone walked into your kitchen and told you that you were suffering from an overdose of self-pity?'

'Awful.'

'Well, then.'

'Perhaps that is the very thing you needed to say and that she needed to hear.'

'How can I be sure of that?'

'Did you intend to tell her that?'

'No, the words just came out.'

'Had you diagnosed that self-pity was the problem?'

'No, I hadn't realised that it was.'

'Where did the knowledge come from, then?'

'From God?'

'Who else?'

'How can I be sure?'

'You can't. You have to trust. You didn't want to hurt Molly; in fact you felt a great love for her and you told me that you prayed that you would say the right things.'

It seemed fruitless to continue the conversation. 'It sounds all right when you put it like that, Tom. Only time can tell whether I have helped or hurt her.'

'Yes, only time can tell. So let's use that time to pray for her.'

When Christopher returned to the rectory, he was surprised to see that Molly was behind with the lunch, particularly as she had not been in the hall for coffee after the service. She answered his queries as to her health and feelings with an icy coldness that sent Christopher scuttling to the sanctury of his study, to await the summons to eat. He buried himself in the Sunday paper, but the news was no more inviting than the reception from his wife.

Molly worked with outward efficiency, being driven by the ice-cold fury within her. Ann's remark had hit home and she hated her for it. Yes, hated. That was the only word for it: coming into her home, holding her, professing love for her and then driving a sharp knife into her heart. If this was the love of God, then Molly Dean would stop her search for Him.

They ate lunch in almost complete silence. 'What did you think of the sermon this morning?' asked Christopher.

'I didn't hear a word of it.'

'You seemed to be listening.'

'Were you preaching at me, then?'

'Don't be silly, of course not.'

'I'm sorry that I'm so silly. I don't have the understanding and perception of your new friends.'

'What do you mean?'

'It doesn't matter.'

'I want to know.'

'It doesn't matter.'

With that she left the table and began the washing up, leaving him to finish his sweet alone.

David Buckley joined Christopher, Tom and Ann the following Tuesday. Since both Ann and Christopher had spent a great deal of time thinking about Molly, she was the obvious topic of conversation.

Ann was surprised that Christopher seemed to know nothing of the encounter with Molly on Sunday morning. He, for his part, was inwardly angry that Ann had taken such a step without first consulting him; then he realised that this was probably part of the Lord's plan to help Molly. He seemed impotent himself in the matter and unable to communicate with his own wife.

'I don't know the answer,' he admitted. 'I feel sure that God knows what he is doing. If I didn't believe that I couldn't stand back and watch her suffer like this. There is something terrible going on within her; I can sense that much.'

'You will have a new wife once it is resolved,' promised Tom. 'We went through something similar, although nothing as deep and far-reaching, of course.'

'I wonder whether she needs help from somebody who has more experience in these things than we have,' said Christopher.

'Do you really think she would accept help at present?' asked Ann.

'I don't know. I don't even know who could help her. It may seem an awful thing to say, but I don't know any of my colleagues locally who would know how to deal with the problem. I think I could—if she were not my wife.

It seems difficult to change roles from a husband to a counsellor.' Tom understood and nodded.

'What do you think the real problem is?'

Christopher thought for a moment. 'Well, I'm not sure. I've prayed a great deal about it. Without talking to her I couldn't be certain I'm right, but . . .' He paused as if aware that he would have to choose his words very carefully. 'I believe that she blames God for all the hurt she has known in her life. So although her surface mind is prepared to accept Him, deep down she doesn't really want to get near Him. At times she probably hates Him.'

'How does the self-pity fit in— or does it?' inquired Ann.

'Oh, it fits in all right. Very much so. I don't think Molly is aware of her schizophrenic approach to God. She is aware of her feelings, and what she feels is self-pity. You see, for years she has led a surface kind of existence, burying the hurts of past years. She could accept God in that way, and even felt accepted by Him. Yet it was all superficial. Now she is forced into reality. And the reality of the situation is that the true Molly Dean feels very sorry for herself because all her life, until she met me at any rate, she was pushed from pillar to post, nobody ever accepting her or loving her. She felt totally rejected and God was to blame.'

'He didn't cause any of the hurt,' said Ann indignantly.

'But He didn't prevent it either,' answered Christopher. 'That is the crucial point as far as Molly is concerned.'

'So how do we help her?' asked Tom.

'I can't,' Christopher replied flatly. 'She can only relate to me in the way that she has always known me. That involved burying the past hurts; they have never been part of our life together. Molly has tried to construct a new life for herself, yet underneath that is this shaky foundation of what she really is. She feels that the superstructure has now been removed and the Molly that is exposed is the one that she has successfully hidden for many years: cold, bitter resentful, and yet desperate for love.'

'Why can't she accept that God loves her?' It was so difficult for Ann to understand how anybody could reject the answer to their problems, especially when they were of such magnitude.

'Because this God is the One who allowed all this hurt in her life.'

'He provided you for her,' commented Ann.

'Yes. That was fine until now.'

They seemed to have reached an impasse. 'Is there no way that we could reach with the love of Jesus into her past life?' It was David Buckley who had spoken. The others had forgotten his quiet presence, being carried away by their concern for Molly.

'How do you mean?'

'I'm not sure. I'm newer at all this than you are. It seems to me that we need to pray for Mrs. Dean as she was—the frightened, unloved, unwanted little girl.'

'You're right,' said Tom enthusiastically. 'It's the hurt little girl who needs healing, who needs Jesus.'

Christopher looked concerned. It sounded feasible, but he had never come across such a suggestion before. Anyway, the prognosis might be correct, but how to effect it was another problem. He expressed his uncertainty.

'At least we can pray in a different way for her,' said Ann. Without more ado, she closed her eyes and began. 'O Lord, you know everything about Molly; more than we do. We know that you love her, even if she cannot accept that for herself. We ask, dear Jesus, that you heal all these past wounds and bring her to the point where, instead of blaming you for the hurt inflicted upon her by others, she greets you as her Saviour. Yes, Lord, in all the wounded areas of her life, we ask that your love may abound. Amen.'

The three men murmured their 'Amens'. If they had been asked, none of them would have been able to confess much faith that the prayer would be answered. At least they understood the problem a little better now. Ann was more confident. 'Remember, God wants us to pray, not because He likes to hear the sound of our voices, but because He wants to answer our prayer!'

They could not argue with that.

When Christopher returned home that evening, Molly was already in bed and asleep. He decided to have a glass of warm milk before joining her. The one great truth about God that was sustaining him through these difficulties was that the Lord loved him. By abiding in the Vine he was directly in the path of His giving. He knew that if he lived his life in faithful obedience to God, depending on His grace, he would discover how great is His desire to give to His children, how overwhelming His generosity.

At this moment he felt very alone. Was this how Molly felt all the time? And without knowing the love of God? He shuddered. It was all beyond him. God was the only answer; there could be no other. The only way to God's heart was prayer. Surely the Spirit would know how to pray?

He knelt on the hard kitchen floor, rested his arms on a hard kitchen chair, and buried his face in his hands. He prayed quietly in tongues for a very long time.

13

THE LAST OF the visitors had gone. Christopher carried the tray of dirty cups into the kitchen and began to wash them. He had a great deal to think about. It had been another evening of revelation for him as well as for the rest of the group. All had listened attentively as he went over what was now familiar ground to him: the picture of the Vine. Yet Christopher was impressed at how new and fresh it was, even to him; there were so many new elements that he hadn't realised before.

There was no doubting the fact that the message was coming across loud and clear. The others were obviously having their struggles, and he was surprised at the openness that was displayed when they had a time of discussion. Young David Buckley had given a simple account of his time with Tom and Ann last Saturday. At first Christopher was worried about the way in which this would be received, but the obvious enthusiasm that David displayed had delighted most. Tom and Ann were seen in a new light, and the ladies were certainly impressed with the simplicity with which Ann spoke about the battle within her that had to be faced before she came into the freedom of the Holy Spirit.

His only bad moment had been when Mrs. Baker asked

why Molly hadn't joined the group. He had tried to laugh the question to one side by saying that she was concerned about their physical comfort as well as their spiritual welfare and that she was preparing the coffee. But neither Mrs. Baker nor any of the others were fooled, and he wondered if it wouldn't have been much more honest to state simply that she didn't want to come, and let them make of that what they would.

One of the things that Christopher had never grasped very clearly was the meaning of the glory of God. He had been surprised, therefore, to find himself talking about it as he expounded verse 8. As he dried the cups he tried hard to remember what he had said.

'A Christian can only have one ambition in life: to glorify the Father. Any other ambition that cuts across that is a wrong ambition. To glorify God is to add to His glory. We shall not be able to do that by opposing His will, only by fulfilling it. He is glorified when His purpose is worked out in the lives of His children.

'Even Jesus said, "I do not seek my own glory. I honour my Father." Any glory that the Son received was given Him by the Father. So He could pray at the climax of His earthly life, "Father, the hour has come; glorify thy Son that the Son may glorify thee." In other words He was saying, "Father, let your purpose be perfectly worked out in me, that you may be glorified in me, that I may share your glory." He prayed, "I glorified thee on earth, having accomplished the work which thou gavest me to do." That is the prayer which we all need to be able to pray. How can we accomplish the Father's purpose for us unless we are prepared to yield ourselves completely into the Father's hands, that His Spirit may bear all the fruit in our lives that He desires to see?'

It was at that point that Vanessa White had broken

145

down. She sat in the far corner of the lounge and quietly wept. Nobody had been certain what to do at first. Then Ann calmly went over to her, squatted on the floor beside her chair and held her hand. In recent weeks Christopher had seen more tears than in as many years. There was a great deal of sadness within people that needed to be released, sadness that had never been touched by the hundreds of sermons he had preached at St. Gabriel's.

All Vanessa could say through the tears was, 'I want Him, I want Him.' She had only been a member of Christopher's congregation for a few months. At last she could express why she had first come to St. Gabriel's. She wanted God. Now, at last, he could lead her to Him. She had stayed behind when the others left. She opened her life to God, bringing into the light the sins that had left her carrying a burden of guilt. As this was lifted from her she became aware of peace flooding in, and the infusion of the Holy Spirit brought joy. The great hug that she gave Christopher before she left the rectory was a spontaneous gesture that said more than any word of thanks that he had received throughout his ministry. Thank God she had been freed to show her gratitude! A new warmth and a new love were creeping into the lives of people—and that is what God wanted them to be—a people of love. If they could love with His love, then God would indeed be glorified in their lives.

Christopher dried the last mug and hung the tea-towel on the hot-water pipe to dry. Molly had gone to bed early again and, being tired, he decided he wouldn't stay up any longer. What a difference in their tiredness, though! As he climbed the stairs he remembered the close association between husband and wife in the Scriptures, the unbelieving one being consecrated through the believing partner.

He felt reassured once more about his wife. As he got into bed, he leaned across and kissed Molly's cheek. 'Molly, I love you dearly.' She gave no indication whether she heard his whisper. But then God had been speaking to her in a still, small voice, and this too had been drowned by her fears and resentment.

The next morning, in his time of quiet before breakfast, Christopher studied Christ's concept of the Church as shown in his prayer of chapter 17 of John's Gospel. 'I in them and thou in me, that they may become perfectly one, so that the world may know that thou hast sent me and hast loved them even as thou hast loved me.'

Christopher could hardly believe his eyes. He had read this passage countless times without ever facing the implications of what Jesus was saying. He had previously interpreted it as a prayer that there should be no disunity or divisions between Christians. To understand His words in terms of relationships brought them into new light. And this was clearly the context in which they were spoken. Jesus was praying that the disciples would know such unity within relationships that they would reflect the relationship of oneness between Father and Son.

Jesus did not pray impossible or fatuous prayers. Presumably, therefore, He meant what He said.

The people of St. Gabriel's hardly knew one another, let alone displayed such a unity in their lives. It was obvious that the unity within the Godhead was one of love, and they would only know such unity if they were filled with God's love. Jesus prayed 'that they may all be one'. Why? 'That the world may believe that thou hast sent me.'

No wonder they had never made much headway with evangelism at St. Gabriel's! The world was fed up with hearing Christians claim that God is love; it needed to see love being lived in the lives of local congregations, in the relationships that existed between Christians. Yet so often the Church appeared to be more like a filing system. People filed into the church building on a Sunday, did their worship thing and then filed out again. The wonder was that people like Vanessa, who wanted God, should hold on long enough in such a system before they found Him. But for every Vanessa, how many slipped away disillusioned, still lost in a fog of despair?

'We have a lot to answer for,' muttered Christopher to himself. 'God forgive us.'

Deep within him the vision was forming of what St. Gabriel's needed to become: a group of people filled with the Spirit of God's love, working that love out in their relationships with one another and reaching out with that love into the lives of those around them. You cannot force people to love. So all this would need to develop, and he must be careful not to push people too fast. God the Holy Spirit was to lead, not Christopher Dean.

The phone rang. Paul Rivers wanted to talk, and said he would be round that evening. As he breakfasted hurriedly Christopher wondered about Paul's attitude to the whole matter. He was going to play an important part in the future development of St. Gabriel's; of that Christopher felt certain. They would need, therefore, to build on the friendship which had deepened over the past years.

Paul came straight to the point. 'Claude Winter has been on to me, Christopher. He says that it's my responsibility as churchwarden to see that the congregation isn't led astray.'

'Is that all he says?'

'Well, no. He implies that you must be suffering from overwork and strain and that the Bishop should relieve you of your duties until you are restored to normal health.'

'I've never felt better,' said Christopher truthfully.

'You would probably have a hard job convincing our friend Claude of that.'

'What do you intend to do about the letter?'

'Obviously, I have no intention of writing to the Bishop. But if I don't Claude probably will.'

'The prospect doesn't alarm me in the slightest. I would welcome the opportunity of talking to the Bishop about what is happening, and the vision that God is giving us for St. Gabriel's.'

'That's why I'm here, Christopher. I want you to share that vision with me. All that you've been saying these last two weeks has been very impressive. In fact, it hasn't really been you speaking, if you see what I mean. I am left, though, with this question: Where is it all leading us?'

'We shall have to talk about that in the group, of course. I don't mind telling you what I can see now, Paul. But understand that all this is only being formulated in my mind at present; there is much I still don't understand, myself.'

'I accept that, but I would still like to know more of your vision. It will help me in dealing with Claude or anyone else who may question me. Already there's quite a lot of speculation in some quarters.'

'I suppose that's inevitable. You can see from what I've been saying that all of us need a personal renewal of our lives.'

'Speak English, man,' said Paul.

'We need to know the Lord in a personal way, to be aware that we have been incorporated into Jesus and are filled with His Holy Spirit.'

'That's fine. So where do we go from there? What happens when more of St. Gabriel's are filled with the Spirit? That's what I want to know.'

'I believe God has been supplying the answer during these past few days.'

'So?'

'We are going to be Jesus!'

'I beg your pardon? Many more statements like that and I shall think seriously about acceding to Claude's request!' He spoke in obvious good humour.

'I'm being serious, Paul.'

'Then you'll have to explain.'

'St. Paul calls the Church the Body of Christ. Right?'

'Right.'

'What does that mean? Surely that the Church is to be Christ's Body in the world, the body of people who continue the ministry of Jesus, preaching, teaching and healing in His name. Is that done effectively at St. Gabriel's? Of course not. We're incapable of it.'

'Shall we ever be capable?'

'This is what we have been called to be and to do. I can't see the purpose of the local church community unless we're determined to do it effectively.'

'How, Christopher?'

'We shan't be able to minister Christ very effectively in perpetuating the kind of life we have now. The whole of our way of church life has to change. I'm not sure yet about all the implications of that, but I can see some of them.'

'Go on. You are being most irritating. Get to the real point.'

'We are only going to minister Jesus to the world around us if we are empowered to do so. Hence the need for every member of St. Gabriel's to be filled with the Holy Spirit. He will provide us with an increase of love in our lives and we are going to become integrated in some way so that we work in harmony and co-operation—like the limbs of a

150

human body. And Christ needs to be the Head of the Body, so that every limb is controlled by Him.'

'It sounds more like a dream than a real proposition.'

'It's what Jesus Himself prayed for.' Christopher then told Paul of the new understanding that he had received through the prayer of John 17. 'Relationships that reflect the love the Father has for the Son; that's only possible through the Holy Spirit.'

'Look at the bickerings and squabblings you see in most churches,' said Paul. 'And St. Gabriel's has its share. You don't have to see any further than this present business with Claude.'

'I know, I know, Paul.'

'Do you really believe this will all happen?'

'It has to . Otherwise, what is the purpose of St. Gabriel's?'

'I can see now why you told me that some would leave.'

'No doubt they will, Paul. Some will not want this life of love and unity with others. Their reticence must not be allowed to prevent us becoming what God wants us to be.'

'How are you going to get everyone to see this?'

'It'll take time. Don't worry! I'm not going to tell them all from the pulpit on Sunday.' Christopher had to laugh at the shocked expressions he imagined on many faces. 'First things first. We'll need to bring many more people to the point of giving their lives to God and allowing Him to give them His life. We can't proceed any further until that has happened.'

'People like me, you mean.'

Christopher smiled. 'Is it such a bad idea?'

'No, it's a very good idea. You don't mind if I wait until my vision has become clearer until I take this step, though?'

'Of course not, Paul. It wouldn't be right to rush anyone. God has waited long enough for us to see what He wants. I expect He is prepared to be patient a little longer until we accept His wishes.'

'One thing worries me, though. You speak as though we are not the Body of Christ now. Yet every week in our worship we state clearly that we are His Body.'

'So we are. But who would think it to look at us! Anybody coming into our fellowship should be able to see that relationships of deep love exist between us. Many non-believers would desire to know Christ if they could see that He had that effect on people's lives. And I have the feeling that many people in our locality with particular needs would be attracted to St. Gabriel's because they knew they would find love and acceptance among us. That doesn't happen at the moment. You know, Paul, in my work here I come across so many people who have a common problem; they need to be loved. I want to say to them, "Come to St. Gabriel's; you will find the love you need there." I can't, because the love isn't there. Not yet, anyway. I believe that there are sufficient of us who want that love in our lives, and so I believe also that we will become the body of love that we need to be.'

'Christopher, I'm sorry that I even doubted you.'

'I wasn't aware that you did.'

'Yes, I have to confess that I couldn't see where all this was getting us. The implications are probably even more far-reaching than you have outlined. Even if we are the Body of Christ, I don't believe He gets much glory out of the fact.'

'Not yet, Paul.'

The two men smiled at one another. Paul stood up and extended his hand towards Christopher. 'We are together in this.'

'Paul, I don't want to shake your hand. I want to hug you like a brother.'

152

Paul Rivers went home, sat down and began to write:

I cannot explain any reason for it, yet I feel happier than I can ever remember feeling. All the way home I wanted to sing. If I had not been so conspicuous I would have skipped, or even danced, instead of walking. Not quite the becoming thing for a middle-aged churchwarden! Everything you said to me made so much sense, and somehow assenting to it all has produced this great joy in me. I haven't prayed to be filled with the Holy Spirit, but I wonder if that has happened. Certainly, I am prepared to give my life whole-heartedly to our good Lord and if He can make me part of such a fellowship of love as you outlined just now I shall indeed be filled with joy. I only wish that my dear wife was still alive to share in the wonder of this moment. If she was, I don't suppose I should need to sit and write this to you, Christopher. I must confess that I've been subject to times of great loneliness recently. I know that I have a need for loving relationships, but it will not be easy to surrender myself to them. If dear Emily experiences eternally the joy that I now feel, then I thank my dear Father in heaven for taking her to Himself.

My dear brother, for you are indeed such, I want to assure you of my affection, my support and my prayers at all times. Talk to me and help me, and I promise to give you whatever counsel I can. I'm sure you realise that to effect the vision you have for St. Gabriel's is going to produce some very difficult times for you personally. I wonder where dear Molly is in all this. She has been conspicuous by her absence, and that must be a hard cross for you to shoulder at present. I didn't like to raise the matter when I was with you. Let me know if I can be of any help in that direction. Emily and Molly

were very close and I have grown fond of her myself.
Somehow I should like to help, if at all possible.

Please excuse the formality of a letter. I have needed
to write this. I wonder if I shall sleep tonight. Loneliness
has been a problem at night, but this evening there
seems to be a Presence, not an absence—a wonderful
Presence, who assures me and comforts me and causes
me to rejoice. I praise God for what He has done in my
life through you, Christopher. May the Father be glorified by the fruit He is allowed to bear in our lives.

> Yours in Him,
> Paul

Christopher rejoiced when he read the letter. He himself
had just experienced another lonely night.

14

CHRISTOPHER OPENED HIS diary to the day's date. The only
entry so far consisted of three letters—A.G.M.—the
Annual General Meeting of the church, an occasion on
which he should sum up the past year, financial, constitu-
tional and spiritual, and outline the future as he saw it.

His diary had become quite important to Christopher.
It was no longer a mere list of commitments and reminders
to reassure him that he was a very busy man and must

therefore be fulfilling his obligations as rector. Each event could now be considered in the context of a forward movement, and gained meaning from its position in the sequence. It was not a question of isolated endeavour, taking two steps in the dark and then trying another direction. Each page was covered with tiny writing as Christopher tried to sum up for himself the past few weeks, and as he considered his address for the evening, he ran his eye over some of the entries ...

Thurs. 29th—The Thursday teaching meeting. It was decided to finish this series tonight as so many of the original members have been baptised in the Spirit and spend Tuesday evening with Tom, Ann and myself. At least six more interested, so will re-start the series with these next week.

Tues. 10th—Attendance reached twenty for the first time at the Tuesday meeting. New dimensions of prayer and praise opening up all the time, and a great spirit of rejoicing in the Lord's presence. Praying in the Spirit and prophecy now in common use, and singing in tongues happened for the second time tonight, in addition to the singing of our growing repertoire of simple songs. Many wish to bring this into the general worship of the church, but can see that over-enthusiasm may cause members of the congregation to retreat. If the others can't see Jesus in our lives without this, there must be something wrong!

Sun. 15th—Realised suddenly this morning how worship in church is slowly changing. Audience participation increased by about 200 per cent. So, incidentally, has the offering. More and more Bibles being brought to parish communion and some of them look quite well used. Boookstall turnover increasing rapidly, Ben informs me. Sermon longer than usual, but this did not deter many from staying behind and talking in small groups scattered around the church, praying and discussing things together. Most encouraging thing is the number of visitors and 'fringe members' who come in, some invited, others just curious. Work-mates, neighbours and relatives are obviously noticing the power of the Spirit in our lives. Many of these are also being brought along on a Tuesday. Rumours to the effect that Claude Winter considers this subversive. Have been at great pains to treat everyone alike, but Claude is creating an impression that there are first- and second-class Christians, counting himself among the latter and inciting revolution.

Tues. 24th—Another joy-filled meeting. Our love for each other now being expressed physically, with a hug instead of a handshake. Growing openness to each other and desire to share our experiences, praising God for answered prayer. Discovered that some of the women are meeting mid-week for prayer and Bible study. When I think how I have been afraid to suggest this sort of thing from the pulpit—and now they go beyond my hopes!

Fri. 27th—During many of my visits, especially to the older members of the congregation, I hear not only thoughts but actual phrases that I am sure originate with Claude. How can I make it clear that I respect these dear people and their form of worship so patiently adhered to for fifty years? Apparently my comments about the necessity of more commitment to a lay ministry have got back to Claude, who wants to make out that I can no longer fulfil my pastoral obligations and should be replaced.

Christopher pushed his diary away and closed his eyes. Through all the joy he felt in seeing God at work among His people, there was a rumble of threat from Claude. He

156

had never come out into the open, and whenever Christopher had considered having it out with him, the Lord had given him a definite 'No'.

Surely tonight the whole thing had to come to a head. In reviewing his hopes for the church, Christopher would have to nail his colours to the mast, and the period of open discussion afterward, always the highlight of Claude's year, would give him unparalleled opportunity for open opposition. Short of denying Claude his rights there was no solution. Yet Paul, Tom and Ann had prayed with Christopher the previous night about this, and all had been filled with peace and a deep love for Claude.

'I'll concentrate on my talk, and if I honour the Lord in that I know He'll look after the rest,' reasoned Christopher, and settled down to do just that.

He had barely begun when the door opened and Molly came into the room. Christopher looked up inquiringly.

'Christopher, I want to talk to you. It won't take very long. I know you probably want to be quiet now, but it can't wait.'

She was obviously in some distress.

'I love you Christopher. No, don't interrupt, please. This isn't very easy for me. It's funny, we've lived together all these years, and now I find it difficult to talk to you.' She tried to smile, but it was a thin, tight-lipped smile that reflected the tension within her. 'I know how hard you've been working recently and the strain you've been under, especially with all this Winter business. I want to say I'm sorry, darling. I'm sorry for the way I've failed you.' She bit her lip in an effort to hold back the tears. 'All through our marriage, I've supported you and encouraged you and now when you have needed me most I've just been another tension in your life.'

Christopher wanted to put his arms around her and re-

assure her; he sensed that he must allow her to finish all
that she wanted to say.

'Last night I was so jealous and so angry with myself
when you were praying with Paul and the Billings. I wanted
to be in here with you. I belonged by your side, not stuck
in the lounge like a deserter. It made me see things more
clearly, though I am no better than Claude myself.'

'Really, Molly!' broke in Christopher.

'Please let me finish. I repeat I am no better than Claude
Winter. I may not have gone around saying the things he
has said, but I've thought them. At least I've thought many
of them—about you, my husband. I need you to forgive
me, Christopher.'

'It's not a question of needing my forgiveness,' he tried
to reassure her.

'Yes, it is. I need your forgiveness and I need it now.
Things can never be right between us until I receive it.'

He had never known her so strong or determined.

'All right, my darling, I forgive you.' He went to embrace
her; the words didn't seem enough.

'No, dear. Wait. I still haven't finished.' She paused, uncertain quite how to continue. She slumped into the chair,
staring down at her feet. Her voice now seemed remote.
'I've been going through a private war of my own in these
last weeks, and I'm afraid the battle isn't over yet. I only
wish it was. I must have been awful to live with—cold and
contemptuous. It was only last night that I realised that
my coldness was not really directed at you, but at God.
You know, I have hated God, I have felt so bitter and
twisted towards Him—all because of the past, of course. I
don't suppose I need to explain it all. Anyway, I feel jealous
and resentful towards all these people who have been
filled with the Spirit. They seem to receive so easily what I

have been striving for all these years—a peace and security with God as well as with my husband. Now I realise that I can never find that peace while there is any trace of hatred or bitterness in me.'

'There still is?'

'Yes, there still is. I can't simply remove it. However, now I know it's there and I don't want it to be there. That, at least, is a start.'

'It's a great step forward, Molly.' Christopher felt a great tenderness for her. 'I too have felt excluded. I've known something of the agony going on within you and I've wanted to help. You haven't allowed me anywhere near you.'

'When you have corns you don't invite people to come and tread on them, even your husband.' Christopher laughed and it wasn't long before Molly joined him. Suddenly, she stood up and flung her arms around him; 'Oh, forgive me, forgive me!'

'I have, I have, my love.'

'It's so good to be held again, to feel your warmth. I've been frozen for months.'

'It's all over now.'

She said nothing in response, but just clung to him, delighting in the sensation of his fingers being run through her hair. After a while, she gently disengaged herself.

'It's not all over, dear, and we both know it. The problem within me is still unresolved. At least we can face that together now. I still don't understand all that is happening here. I've wanted to reject it, I've wanted to believe that Claude was right. But I can't reject it; it's all too real to people and it's infuriating, but I can see the fruit you're always on about.' The smile was warm and full this time. 'Anyway, Claude is as big and pompous an ass as he ever was.'

'Molly!'

'Well, he is! And to think I wanted to agree with him! I must have been mad.'

'Not mad, just hurt. There are some things deep in you that need healing, dear. That may take a little time. Eventually, you too will know the Lord's love and joy and when you do—boy, you'll be great to live with.'

They laughed and hugged briefly. 'Now's not the time,' said Molly. 'I must leave you to be quiet. I'm sorry to have taken your time. At least we can take on Claude together,' she laughed.

'I trust the Lord will be involved too.'

'I wouldn't know about that—yet.' Molly shut the door. It had been a long time since Christopher had heard her singing around the house.

The first part of the meeting had followed its familiar pattern. Claude had seated himself in the second row, to one side. He wouldn't be too conspicuous while seated, yet in easy view of both Christopher and the rest of the assembly when he rose to speak. The hall was full. There was an air of expectancy as Christopher rose to give his address.

'Praise be to God our Father, to our Lord Jesus Christ and to His blessed Holy Spirit for all the wonders of His love that He has poured into our lives during the past year! St. Peter prays "that in everything God may be glorified through Jesus Christ. To Him belong glory and dominion for ever and ever. Amen." ' Several people echoed the 'Amen'.

Christopher continued: 'It is the bearing of much fruit that will prove to the world that we are disciples of Jesus. The Church has only talked about the love of God for too long. People need to see God in the lives of Christians and they have every right to expect to be able to do so. Has anyone ever said to you, "I would believe in your God if I could see Him"? How do you answer such a question? "God is a Spirit. You can't see Him, but you have to believe that He's here."

'This is totally unconvincing. Surely we should be able to say, "If you want to see God, come with me." In the church at worship, he or she should be conscious of the power of God's presence among His people, and be able to see God's love in the relationships that exist between them, relationships such as can be found nowhere else in the world. Sadly, that is far from the case at present.' Christopher glanced at Claude Winter. The latter sat with his head bowed. He was giving nothing away.

'There are so many ways in which we need to be offering Jesus to the people around us. First to those who come seeking the reality of God; then reaching out, getting our hands dirty in the mess of other people's lives, just as the Lord delighted in being the servant of God among men, yet offering not only love and compassion, but also the healing power of Jesus, the transforming life of the Holy Spirit to change these situations, to ease the desperation in the hearts and lives of so many.

'How can we be made ready for such things, unless we allow God Himself to equip us? That He is prepared to do. He has already shown us this quite clearly. Many of us still feel unable to give to others because we have received so little ourselves from God. Our poverty is not the result of His meanness, for He is longing to give us His riches.

'Fruit is going to be produced in our lives, fruit that will last, fruit that will be produced through the activity of God's Holy Spirit within us. Then God will be glorified and honoured. I don't believe we have learned yet what it is to live for Him. We need to allow God to fill our lives

161

and then guide us into the use of His love and power. Until now in my ministry such words would have had no real meaning. Now I can see that we can live them, because of all the Holy Spirit is doing among us.'

Christopher stole another quick look in Claude's direction. He sat motionless as before.

'That is what the year ahead holds for us: learning to love one another without judgment or criticism so that others may be drawn into this community of love. I, for one, am a little afraid of what that may mean. I have always liked to think of myself as independent and self-possessed. I need to love others, but I have not wanted them to get very close to me. Yet it is the one who receives love who gives love. To give or to receive will often involve denying ourselves.

' "Whoever does not bear his own cross and come after me, cannot be my disciple," said Jesus. Being a disciple is a costly business. The cross is the way of self-denial and complete obedience to the Father. If we are "in Christ" then presumably we are prepared to let Him dictate the terms and forget any rights we may think we have to our opinions and ideas.

'Jesus knew well that many would be prepared to accept Him as Saviour; few would want to acknowledge Him as Lord. When He had difficult things to say, He had to watch sadly while some of His disciples turned away from Him.

'Several of us have already asked our heavenly Father to take hold of the whole of our lives and graft us into the Vine of Jesus. He has done that, and everything that we are, and potentially ever could be, is placed in Him. As we live our lives together in Him, we shall need to leave behind many of our worldly ideas and ambitions.

'Yet God obviously has a great deal to give to us—not

162

only from above, but through one another. This will involve a life of sacrifice and self-denial, but a life also of great blessing. We are faced once again with that divine principle of giving. The Lord desires that we give freely to Him; He then freely and lovingly gives immeasurably more back to us. There may be misunderstanding, rejection, even persecution now; yet we shall be held safe in God's life and love.

'I, for one, have had to face the hard fact that it is often those who are closest to us who find it most difficult to understand our commitment to Christ. They sometimes feel rejected, although as the love of God fills our hearts, we feel an increasing love for them. It is that power of love that will prevail. That same love that took Jesus to the cross.

'At the time when I consent to the Father taking hold of my life and placing me in the Vine, I am acknowledging all that the Father has already done for me in Jesus. I am appropriating the fruit of His life and of His sacrifice of love. I, in turn, take my place in the Vine, that my life may be a living sacrifice through which God will bear much fruit to His glory.'

Christopher sat down. There was silence. No one stirred. Nobody coughed. When he looked up, he realised that nearly everyone was praying.

If anybody had come to the meeting expecting high drama, they must have gone away very dissatisfied. After Christopher's speech any other discussion would have seemed irrelevant and the meeting ended quietly when the prayers were concluded.

What drama there was was reserved for a few. Claude Winter had remained speechless all evening. Only when the gathering was dismissed and people began stacking the chairs did it become obvious that Claude Winter was unconscious—and had been for some time. Soon before the speech began, he had suffered a stroke.

Most people were well clear of the hall by the time the ambulance arrived. Christopher, Molly and Paul followed to the hospital. There was nothing they could do except await news of his condition, and pray. In all three a deep fear lurked. Was this the hand of God? Was this His judgment for Claude's opposition to the working of His Holy Spirit? Was this His answer to their prayer that he should be made speechless and so unable to interfere with the meeting?

They sat silently in the waiting-room with the same questions nagging away within them. If he died, who would mourn him? He had never married and had few real friends. If only he could have seen how much he would have gained through St. Gabriel's becoming truly a family of love!

' "I will wound and I will heal," ' muttered Christopher.

'Pardon?' said Paul.

'I was thinking of a word from the Old Testament: "I will wound and I will heal." '

'Do you think this is the Lord's doing?' asked Molly.

'I honestly don't know. And I don't think this is the time to work that one out. Even if it is the Lord who has wounded, there is still the promise, "I will heal." '

'Lord,' Paul prayed, 'we don't know what to make of all this. Last night you gave us a love for Claude. That's why we're here now. We love him and we care about him. If this is some kind of judgment upon him, we ask you to have mercy on him now; give him time to repent, and touch him with your healing power.'

The duty doctor entered the room as Paul finished the sentence.

'You are friends of Mr. Winter?'

164

'Yes,' said Christopher, 'I'm his rector.'

'Do you know who his next of kin is?'

'No. I'm afraid not. He isn't married. I believe he has an aged mother in a home somewhere. He didn't speak of her very much and as far as I know didn't visit her often either. How is he?'

'He was in a critical condition when he arrived. It is too early to be definite yet, but he seems to have a fairly strong constitution.'

'You can say that again,' said Molly.

The doctor managed a smile. 'I thought you were a friend of his.' Molly felt about as high as a thimble and thoroughly ashamed of herself.

'I'm sorry,' she murmured. 'Neither he nor I have been very charming people recently.' She managed to look the young man straight in the eye. 'Please forgive me.'

It was his turn to retreat. 'It is no concern of mine. Please excuse me.'

'Is there anything more we can do here?' Christopher called after him.

'Nothing, thank you,' he said crisply, 'unless you would like to finish your prayer meeting. Good night.' With that he was gone.

'What an objectionable young man,' commented Paul.

'I seem to remember saying something earlier this evening about not being selective in our loving,' grinned Christopher.

'I believe Claude is going to be all right.' Both the men stared at Molly.

'What makes you say that?' asked Paul.

'I don't know. I feel at peace about it—isn't that the right phrase, Christopher?' The three of them laughed together. A good job that the young doctor wasn't still present! He would have doubted the reality of their love for Claude. It was strange how they could feel such concern for him, and yet still have that joy within them.

'Darling, you were terrific this evening. You know, I heard what you said. Until then I hadn't really heard; I'd been receiving all that you were saying through a fog of prejudice and bitterness. I didn't really want to hear or to face up to what was happening around me. Tonight I heard because I wanted to hear. I even want to hear more.'

'Don't give any credit to me, dear. Any inspiration there might have been came from the Holy Spirit.'

'Then tonight you were annointed by the Holy Spirit.'

'That's your opinion, is it?'

'No, it's a fact.'

'Well, fact or not, the words came tumbling out. It seems to be like that whether I'm preaching or speaking at a teaching meeting. Something happens and the words come flowing out.'

'You're a strange man.'

'You're a strange woman—but it's good to have you back.'

'My problem isn't solved, you know. Inside, there is still emptiness.'

'But now you want God to fill that emptiness?'

'I think so.'

'He will.'

'I wish I could believe that more firmly.'

'There is plenty of time . . .'

For the first time for many weeks they did not turn their backs on one another as they drifted into sleep.

15

SUNDAY AFTERNOON AT the Billings' looked far from its usual dozy, over-fed self that week. In family communion Christopher had preached on love, and Tom had been glad to be reminded of some basic issues. He noticed Ann was very quiet on the subject as she prepared dinner, and was quite taken aback by the vehemence of her opinion when it finally came half-way through the second course.

'But Tom, we can't go on and on preaching "new relationships of love" for ever. The psychological problems of Vine living are absolutely minute compared to the real suffering that Christ may ask us to face.'

'What sort of thing are you thinking of, love?' Tom's voice was encouraging: he sensed that Ann's mind was full of thoughts that demanded expression.

'Well, look at the way Christ suffered, simply because He refused to put Himself first, and upheld the truth. And Paul followed closely along the same path. Have you read 2 Corinthians 11? Go and have a look.'

Tom, who was still finishing a baked apple, asked Angela to fetch his Bible from the hall. When she came back he was concentrating on scraping the skin, while still listening to Ann. Angela hovered for a moment. 'Can we leave the table, Daddy?' At his word Tony slipped down from his chair and vanished with Angela. Tom opened the Bible and found the passage in question while Ann packed up dishes around him. By the time he joined her in the kitchen his mind was reeling with beatings, imprisonments, shipwrecks, stonings, hunger and cold, not to mention great pressures of work and the necessity of involvement with hundreds of people scattered over vast areas.

'I see what you mean,' he admitted, feeling humbled. Ann was beginning to make a cake, and since he wanted to continue the conversation he ran the water for the washing up and tackled the job thoughtfully.

'It's no good evangelising people into a lop-sided view of what God is offering,' expounded Ann. 'All right! He gives us eternal life and love, joy and peace. Our sins are forgiven, we gain freedom from doubts and fears. We are learning about all that. But we are also called to a life of self-denial, sacrifice and suffering for the sake of the Gospel. Jesus lost many followers when He preached that truth.' She was pounding butter and sugar together vigorously, and Tom couldn't help wondering whether she had chosen the task on purpose to let out her emotions. There was a pause while she looked for eggs, and Tom swished a brush rather lamely over a plate. Over the cracking of eggshells she began again.

'Jesus knew that He needed to suffer and die for the cause of the kingdom, to bring others to life. How can a true Christian avoid the fact that the same may be required of him?' "Not everyone who says to me 'Lord, Lord' shall enter the kingdom of heaven, but he who does the will of my Father who is in heaven." '

'You'd better stick to cooking,' suggested Tom. 'Your cake is more digestible than your thinking!'

Ann laughed. 'Oh, I haven't finished yet. Is the weighing-pan clean yet? I'll give you one word of comfort, though;

in His love for the Vine the Father won't require more fruit from a branch than it can stand.'

'Thank you for that, anyway.'

'Well, that's obvious, Tom. He doesn't want the branch to snap under the weight. So whatever the Father asks of us is only going to be fulfilled if we abide in the love of Jesus—not our own, of course, because in a crisis that will let us down, and His can never fail. Think about Paul. Whatever the situation, God is saying "Go on living in my love." '

Tom mechanically took the dirty weighing-pan to wash again. 'You mean we can only survive if we are obedient to that?'

'It's not just a question of survival, but we miss the best if we aren't ready to trust. We have the joy of knowing God to be reliable when everything is going well—think what it will mean when we come to the end of our resources and still find Him faithful.'

'And of course in the final run we are inadequate to live the life God wants us to.' Tom paused. 'I wonder what He wants for us now.'

Ann handed the mixing-bowl to Tom. 'I'm sure we haven't missed any boats yet, but I have been faced with the need to accept a challenge, in fact, *the* challenge, when it comes along. It will come, because there is always another challenge ahead.'

'You've obviously spent some time on all this,' said Tom, picking up a tea-towel.

'It started after that Sunday when I went to see Molly. Obviously the thought of becoming a Christian was not so attractive to some people, so I started thinking about it. I study the Bible when you and the children have left the house in the morning, and I've been delving into the cost of becoming a disciple.'

169

'What else have you discovered?'

'Plenty! Don't bother about drying that lot—let's sit down with some coffee.'

'Well?' asked Tom a few minutes later, as he settled into an armchair.

'I suppose it's the attitude of Paul and others to suffering that really challenged me. If Paul could rejoice in prison, who are we to moan that we would rather stay in by the fire than go to a Bible study in the rain? Some blame God as soon as anything goes wrong, some blame the devil. Do you ever hear anyone rejoice? Read 1 Peter, chapter 4.' Tom reached for his Bible.

' "Beloved, do not be surprised at the fiery ordeal which comes upon you to prove you, as though something strange were happening to you. But rejoice in so far as you share Christ's sufferings, that you may also rejoice and be glad when His glory is revealed." '

'You see?' Ann challenged. 'Peter suggests that we can glorify God in suffering for the Gospel, just as Jesus was glorified by the Father when He faced crucifixion. Now try the opening verses of James.'

Tom readily identified the relevant verses. ' "Count it all joy, my brethren, when you meet various trials, for you know that the testing of your faith produces steadfastness." '

'Tom, we live in such conflict: flesh opposed to the spirit, our desires over against the will of God, whether we listen to the opinions of men or the Word of God. That conflict is bound to be there because the world will hate us for what we believe, just as it hated Jesus. It hates us because we have left it behind, turned our backs on its false ways, its false words and ideas, its false values.'

'But we only encounter hatred if we have rejected all that.'

'How could we not reject it, Tom? And having done

that, the only way to withstand successfully is to abide in Jesus. How else could Paul, Peter and James rejoice in their suffering? How else can those who suffer imprisonment and torture for their faith be filled with joy in their adversity?'

'You're preaching, dear!'

'I'm sorry, Tom.'

'It's a frightening prospect, having to suffer for the Lord in the way that some do. That would be a real test of our faith.'

'That's certainly true. Yet look at the way our faith is put to the test in the life of comfort and ease that we have. Not in the same way, of course. In difficulty you know you have to stand by what you believe. It seems that we Christians allow so much of our Lord's teaching to be eroded away by our desire for an easy faith that will give us an easy life.'

'There is ample suffering for us to face around us if we are prepared to, you mean?' asked Tom.

'Yes, so long as we don't mind denying ourselves to be of service to others in the world.'

'The Christian Church has a long history of such service.'

'Thank God that it has! The point is, Tom, that you and I have to work out the implications of all this in our life together. That surely is going to be part of the fruitfulness. As far as I can see, to suffer for Christ means to proclaim him fearlessly by what we are, the way we live, the things we do, wherever the Lord chooses to place us. At present that is right here! Do we really desire to live our whole lives in Christ and for Him? Do we mean it when we say that we want Him to work through us in any way that He desires to further the establishment of His Kingdom on earth?'

There was a pause while Ann went out to check up on

171

the sponge. When she came back, Tom voiced his reservation.

'But, Ann darling, we haven't come up against any opposition yet.'

'I know, Tom, I know. That's the whole point. Where is the love of Jesus in us if we don't experience any opposition?' He could see tears coming to her eyes. 'I'll tell you where it is, Tom. It's there, locked up inside us. All we rejoice in so far is that God has given us so much love. It's time we let that love out and began to share it with those who need it. There's only one problem.'

'What's that?'

'I don't know how. God has given me all this love and I don't know how to share it.'

She rushed past him and up the stairs.

Claude Winter was left speechless after his stroke, his mouth pulled into an ugly shape. His right side was also paralysed and he was unable to write, making communication extremely difficult. For once he had to listen to others.

It was not so much the things that were said that brought about a considerable change in both Claude's health and his happiness. The members of the Tuesday evening prayer meeting decided to pray for Claude daily, and as he had no relatives in the district, to visit him as well. Every afternoon and evening, two members of the group would be at his bedside.

This proved extremely demanding for most of them. Few enjoyed hospital visiting at the best of times and as Claude could not speak, they had to keep up a flow of conversation for half an hour or else sit in embarrassed silence.

At first, Claude did not care much for their talk. It was the fact of their coming that he could not understand: every afternoon two housewives, every evening two of the men. Many who came were those who had been the subject of his harshest criticisms. Yet not one made any reference to this; no one reproached him. They told him about their families, the new police station being built, and read pieces from the newspapers.

Never had such love or concern been shown to him, and as the days passed he began to know his visitors, through having heard so much of their conversation. He became aware that he had never truly listened to anyone before; he had been far too interested in himself and his own opinions. Now he began to look forward to visiting times.

Claude had never quite seen the relevance of prayer; he could not believe that God would intervene in the circumstances of his life. The Lord had equipped him with an intellect and other gifts that it was his job to use to the best of his ability. These visitors obviously believed that God not only could, but also would, change things. They even dared to suggest that He would remove the paralysis from Claude's body and restore his speech.

Christopher was also a regular visitor, choosing times when he could be alone with Claude. Before leaving, he would spend several minutes in prayer, holding his paralysed hand. Claude could discern no physical improvement, although peace descended upon him during these times of prayer, a blessed relief from the turmoil of thinking. He was being made to face many truths about himself and was rapidly coming to the conclusion that he did not like himself very much.

After some days, the visitors suggested spending some of the time reading the Scriptures with him. He was incapable of expressing his true reactions to this offer when it was first made; yet these became precious moments during the visitors' time with him. He had never heard the words before—not in his heart, that was—despite the fact that he had heard hundreds of Bible readings within the context of public worship at St. Gabriel's. Somehow the words were now alive with meaning. At first he thought that this was due to the understanding way in which they were read by his visitors. But long after they had gone, the words still filled his thoughts. He was grateful that one day one of the visitors left a copy of the New Testament in a modern translation on his bedside locker. Soon, he became lost to the activity of the hospital ward, spending much of his waking moments in reading. The book was obviously being well used, a fact that did not go unnoticed by Christopher or the others.

Claude had been in hospital for twenty days and was feeling much stronger, although still physically incapacitated, when Christopher decided that the time was right to speak to him about the healing power of Jesus. Claude heard him out with obvious interest, although only sadness could be seen in his eyes. If only he could talk! It seemed clear to Christopher that he would need to make an act of repentance before coming to the Lord and asking Him for healing. It was difficult to see how that could be done, with an inability to communicate.

Christopher prayed that night, feeling that he had failed in his approach to Claude earlier that afternoon. 'Lord, show us the way to bring your love to Claude's life and body.' On the following morning, Ann telephoned to say that she too had been praying, and believed that the Lord was showing her that the usefulness of Claude's silence was now spent. Christopher asked her to go with him that afternoon.

He explained to the surprised Claude that they believed it right to pray with him and ask God to heal him. Claude seemed almost frightened at the prospect. He pointed to

174

the Testament, which Ann handed to him. With his left hand he turned to the opening chapter of the letter of James. He pointed to verse 26. Christopher read the verse aloud: 'If any one thinks he is religious, and does not bridle his tongue but deceives his heart, this man's religion is vain.'

Ann took hold of his hand. 'God will forgive you,' she said.

He pointed to Christopher. 'Yes, that's right,' Christopher confirmed. Claude waved his hand. Obviously, they had not fully understood. Again, he pointed to Christopher.

'He wants you to forgive him,' said Ann.

Christopher felt a great compassion for the man as he lay there helpless. 'I forgive you, Claude, and I ask you to forgive me for any harsh thoughts that I may have had about you.'

'Thank you. Oh, thank you,' said Claude.

It was a moment or two before either Ann or Christopher reacted. 'Glory to God, you spoke!' said Christopher excitedly. 'Claude!' exclaimed Ann as she instinctively bent over the bed to hug him as best she could.

'Can you say anything else?' asked Christopher.

Claude could only manage an indistinguishable mutter. 'We'll pray,' Christopher said to Ann.

Again she reached for his hand, while Christopher placed his hands on Claude's head. 'Heavenly Father, you are the Lord who heals, and we thank you for this first indication that you want to heal our dear brother, Claude. We ask you now to restore his speech and to lead him to that wholeness of body, mind and spirit that he needs. In the name of your Son, Jesus, we ask this.'

He kept his hands on Claude's head while he continued to pray silently in both tongues and English.

'God, I thank you for my friends.' Both Ann and Christopher opened their eyes at the sound of Claude's voice. 'Oh,' gasped Ann.

'What's the matter?' asked Christopher.

'Look at his mouth.'

Claude's face was restored to normal. The mouth was no longer on an ugly slant. Ann made him look at himself in the mirror.

'I won't get such a shock when I shave now,' he said with a grin. He moved his jaw and other facial muscles, rejoicing in their new-found freedom. 'My face has been a reflection of how I have been inside: ugly and twisted. How can I thank you enough?'

'Don't thank us: praise God for His love and mercy,' answered Christopher.

'I shall do that all right.'

'Is there any sign of movement in your right side?' asked Ann.

'I'm afraid not. It is such a relief to be able to talk again that I really don't mind,' he replied with a chuckle. 'I need to do some talking to you, Christopher. There are a number of things that need to be put right in my life. I think it best if God leaves me in this bed until they have all been resolved. By the way, two days ago the doctor said it was unlikely that I would ever recover my speech properly. He's in for a surprise!'

'I'll leave you two alone if you prefer,' Ann made ready to go.

'No, no, my dear. There is plenty of time to sort me out.' There seemed to be a new softness about Claude, very different from the brash, hard exterior that he used to project. 'To be honest, I want to take this slowly,' he continued. 'You see, I feel as though I am at last climbing out of an enormously deep pit. It has been very dark, and the air has been foul. I'm not out yet, but I can see the top and I can feel the draught of fresh air pouring down upon me. I need to pause for breath, before making the final effort to reach the edge of the pit.'

'You won't arrive there through effort,' said Christopher gently.

'You're probably right. I still need to rest, though. It must be all this talking.'

It was obviously right for Ann and Christopher to leave. As they made their way out of the ward, Christopher could not resist the temptation to stop one of the nurses. 'I think Mr. Winter may have something to say to you.'

As if on cue, Claude's voice rang through the ward. 'Nurse!'

16

THE NEWS THAT Claude Winter had 'changed sides' spread rapidly through the congregation. Those who had been moved by his divisive tactics found themselves without a leader. Returning from hospital, he became a witness for the new life. He lost no opportunity to point out to those who had been swayed by his previous opinions that their attitudes were due to ignorance and fear.

Those who had suffered from Claude's invective were at first suspicious, wary that this might be some new tactic to cause disruption. However, the change that had taken place in his personality was evidence enough that their fears were groundless. It wasn't long before most were forced into a grudging respect for his honesty and openness.

Of greater significance to Christopher, though, was the effect on Molly. She had counted on Claude being more resilient than herself. Her opposition had given way to a genuine search for God, yet there persisted deep within her the thought that she could never prove acceptable to Him. Now she was confronted with the undeniable fact that someone utterly opposed to what was now clearly the Lord's working at St. Gabriel's had been accepted and obviously filled by God with this love that was all around her. If Claude could be received by the Lord, might He not also accept her? The problem was that she still could not accept herself.

Her head told her that what Christopher, Tom, Ann and the others said was true; her heart still insisted otherwise. 'The heart is deceitful above all things, and desperately corrupt: who can understand it?' she read in Jeremiah. Was her own heart deceiving her, and preventing her from sharing the reality of the Lord's joy and peace that she now saw in others?

She longed for the conflict to end, but found the problem painful to talk about, even to Christopher.

Christopher, greatly relieved by her change of attitude, was concerned to take things very gently, fearful that too much pressure would cause a reversion to her former state.

The break-through for Molly came in the most unlikely way. Christopher was preaching a course of sermons on John 15, and had come to verse 10 in the series. 'If you keep my commandments, you will abide in my love, just as I have kept my Father's commandments and abide in His love.'

The phrase stuck in Molly's mind: 'If you keep my commandments you will abide in my love.' This seemed to be the kind of promise that she could understand and accept. What were the commandments that she was to keep? To love God with all her heart, mind, soul and strength? She did not feel any love at all for God. To love her neighbour as herself? She felt no love for herself. Both commands seemed equally impossible. To add to the burden she heard her husband now proclaiming a third. 'This is my commandment, that you love one another as I have loved you.'

'Impossible, impossible!' Molly wanted to shout. 'It's all impossible. Why, I'm not even sure if He loves me. How can I possibly love others with His love when I don't even *know* His love?'

Just then Christopher asked that very question from the pulpit. 'We need to be filled with God's love to enable us to be the people He intends us to be. We need to love one another with the love that He gives us.' The words droned on.

'How? How? How? I can't,' said Molly to herself. She felt a greater failure than ever before. All around her people's lives were being filled with love and here she was, the minister's wife, incapable of love. 'I've only ever loved myself. I've loved Christopher for the security he could give me and for the assurance I feel when I am with him. Is that really love? Her confusion continued.

'If you keep my commandments . . .' Again the words from the pulpit, '. . . you will abide in my love.'

'Oh God, help me. I want to love. I want to give love, not only receive it from others. I want to really love Christopher. 1 want to love all these people around me. I want to love You, Lord. I want to. I want to. Oh, forgive me, forgive me for not loving. I want to love. I want to love.'

The prayer was a silent one for all its intensity, and suddenly there was peace for Molly. No confusion, no turmoil. Only peace. She sat motionless, oblivious of all that was happening around her. 'You will abide in my love.' They were the only words that remained. Now they were being spoken to her. A still, small voice, quite unmistakable 'You will abide in my love.'

She wanted to stand up and shout, 'I can love. I can love.' That God had spoken to her was beyond doubt, and she longed for the sermon to finish so that she could sing, express how she felt. Was this the 'bubble of joy' that the others had spoken about? She would burst unless she was allowed to speak soon.

'To God be the glory, great things He has done.' What a hymn for the occasion! For the first time, Molly had communion with her Lord. Although she had received the sacrament countless times before, this was the first occasion that she had known that unity with Jesus for which she had longed.

Tom and Ann only had to look at Molly to know that their prayers had been answered. They embraced unashamedly at the end of the service.

'You were right, Ann, it was self-pity. For years I have felt unable to give love and I have blamed all that happened to me in childhood for that. I felt sorry for myself and only wanted to be loved. That is why I have treasured Christopher so highly. This morning I realised that I couldn't receive love from God or you, or anybody else, because I was not prepared to give it.'

'You felt you couldn't,' interrupted Tom.

'I know, I know,' continued Molly. 'But don't you see? Once I arrived at the point of wanting to love God and Christopher and you and all the others, God could give me His love. At least, I was able to receive His love.'

'Instead of waiting to be loved all this time, you needed to give love,' said Ann.

'Precisely,' agreed Molly. 'I knew I couldn't, so I had to ask God to supply the love for me to give to Him and to others. And I really believe He has.'

Christopher joined them during the conversation. He was overjoyed. He hugged his wife, quietly praising God for His goodness and patience.

'Darling, there must be so many other people around who are making the same mistake: they sit around waiting to be loved, instead of reaching out in love to others.'

'Perhaps they also feel incapable of giving, as you did, my love.'

'Then they should ask God to give them love.'

They all laughed at the intense expression on Molly's face.

'What are you all laughing at?'

'It's so easy now, Molly. It didn't seem that way earlier this morning.'

As they walked home, Christopher asked, 'Did my sermon help you, dear?'

'Help!' repeated Molly. 'It infuriated me! I almost threw the hymn book at you!'

The following Sunday brought an even greater surprise.

'A member of the church family has something on his heart that he feels he must share with you all,' said Christopher and then returned to his seat as Claude Winter limped to the front of the congregation. He stood silently for a few moments: for once it seemed an effort for him to speak. No one moved.

'Last week, Christopher talked to us about loving and forgiving one another. I have already asked him to forgive me for the damage I caused in the church and for the way

I personally maligned him. He has very graciously forgiven me. However, I feel that I need to ask all of you to forgive me for what I tried to do here. If I had succeeded I would have wrecked a very precious moving of God's Spirit amongst us, and would have deprived you of many blessings. Thankfully, God did not allow me to succeed. Instead I was placed in such a position that I could only gratefully receive all the love that you gave me. I am still profoundly grateful for that. I want you all to forgive me for the way in which I have sinned against this church. I have the Lord's forgiveness, and Christopher's. Now I need yours, and I pray that God will give me the opportunity to love everyone whom I have hurt.'

Claude returned quietly to his place. There was silence; no further sermon was necessary. It was Christopher's turn to be surprised when Paul Rivers stood up and called the congregation to prayer.

'Heavenly Father, we have much pleasure in forgiving our brother Claude in your name. And we pray that this example of openness that he has given us today will lead to a greater love between us all.'

The building echoed with the 'Amen'.

News was obviously circulating in the district about some of the events of recent months, particularly that people were being healed and helped in their problems. Christopher had reached the point in his ministry of despairing over the fact that people no longer seemed willing to turn to the church with their problems. Now the situation was rapidly changing: first a trickle, then a steady flow of people needing help. Many who came were suffering from deep emotional problems, needing to receive a great deal of love and to know that they were accepted, not treated as inadequate members of society.

This was St. Gabriel's greatest challenge. To love the lovely was not particularly difficult. To give of yourself to those who were likely to mistreat your love or even throw it back in your face was another thing altogether. Like most congregations, St. Gabriel's had consisted of people who were keen not to become involved with other people's needs. To be faced with so many simply asking to be loved caused real consternation, even among those newly filled with the Spirit of God. Every one of these 'problems' seemed to demand so much love that the burden of responsibility would need to be shared throughout the body of St. Gabriel's. The problem was staring them straight in the face, not in some abstract sense, but in the flesh and blood of men and women crying out for help and support.

The Lord would need to give the members of St. Gabriel's a continual outpouring of His love. They would need to be healed of their fears and inhibitions in sharing that love with one another, and they would have to be drawn into a ministering body of people, instead of being separate individual Christians trying to do good.

It seemed a daunting prospect; people like Tracy forced them to face it.

Tracy was fourteen, with the physical appearance of someone several years older. One Sunday she came to the morning service and sat in the front pew, as if wanting to be noticed. Her clothes were dirty, her appearance scruffy. Several took a quick look at her and rapidly averted their eyes. There might have been a time when critical comments would have been passed. 'Fancy someone coming to church dressed like that!' Now there was no criticism, only embarrassment.

She appeared to take no part in the service; she simply sat there, glad to be out of the rain and wind for a while.

'How can anyone be so lost at such a young age?' Christopher asked God. He received only silence for an answer. If there was a reply, it was the girl herself—the need to be loved and accepted and helped.

But before he had the chance to talk to her she had slipped away. Christopher was bitterly disappointed that nobody else had tried to befriend her; everyone had left the task to somebody else. Perhaps each hoped that the embarrassing spectacle would not return. However, next Sunday, there she was again, sitting in the front pew. Before the service began, Christopher made a point of talking to her and saying that he would like to speak to her afterwards. She only hung her head and made no reply.

When he went to the pulpit to preach, he was overjoyed that she was no longer sitting alone. Molly, of all people, was next to her. The girl did not seem to acknowledge her presence, sitting in the same listless manner as before. However, her escape route was now made more difficult. When Molly talked to her after the final hymn, the only answer she received was a brusque 'Shut up!' followed by a few murmured words that were fortunately incoherent. Instead of putting her off, Tracy's manner awoke a deep response in Molly. Perhaps she could understand the loneliness of this girl, her desire for love and the intense fear that someone might actually offer her that love. What a trap to be caught in!

It was several minutes before she managed to elicit the girl's name from her. She said that she only wanted to be left alone, and Christopher was hardly more successful than Molly in gathering any further information from her. She was stubborn in her refusal to move, until the church clock struck one. A look of sudden horror came over her face and she rushed out before either of them could ask the cause for her great concern.

During the following week, Christopher made discreet enquiries about the girl and found that her situation was typical of many of her age living on the housing estate. This was the first time that anyone from there had sought help from the church, if that indeed was Tracy's intention. Why was it that people no longer turned to the church to receive the love of God? Christopher knew the answer only too well. He was thankful that Tracy had come, for perhaps this was a sign that something of God's love was at last being manifested through St. Gabriel's.

Apparently she was an unwanted child, her father more often drunk than sober, her mother with men other than her husband. To her parents she could be of no value until she could leave school and earn hard cash. At present she was a parasite demanding food that would only be given her if she fulfilled the duties of a drudge. Much of the housework was considered her responsibility and a good hiding awaited her if her father's food was not immediately ready when he wanted it. Any social worker could point to numerous similar cases that even the concern of the welfare state could not prevent.

This particular case had now become a personal issue to Christopher. How could he talk to Tracy about a God of love, when she had never known genuine affection? How could he tell her that God wanted to be her Father, when such a suggestion could only encourage fear and dread? Perhaps Tracy would not return; he and Molly had seemed very ineffective in their dealings with her on the previous Sunday. He knew better than to barge into the home situation, where his interference would be bitterly resented by Tracy as well as by her parents, and would only cause her further suffering at the hands of her father.

The authorities had been concerned for some time, but no case of cruelty could be proved and there were dozens of Tracys who had been brought to their attention.

However, she did return on the following Sunday and took up her accustomed place—even though Molly had already positioned herself in the front row. That, at least, was a sign of hope. This time she did not attempt to leave, but sat there and talked and talked. She did not look at Molly, but stared straight ahead at the cross which stood behind the altar, speaking her thoughts aloud, pleased that somebody was there to listen and take notice.

'I must go now,' she suddenly said and again departed swiftly.

Week by week, she became more relaxed in her conversation, and even answered some of Molly's questions. Christopher grew accustomed to a much later Sunday lunch, which he did not like; it seemed that many small irritations accompanied the sharing of your life with others in love.

One day, Molly answered the doorbell and was surprised to see Tracy standing on the step. At first she did not recognise her in her school uniform.

'Come in, Tracy.' The girl hesitated, then entered and stood awkwardly in the hallway. 'I have some cooking to do. Come into the kitchen and we can talk there.' Molly led the way.

'What's the matter?'

'Thought I'd come and see yer,' Tracy replied.

'I'm very pleased you have. Let me put the kettle on and we can have a cup of tea.' Tracy sat on a stool and put her school case on the floor.

'She's gone.' Tracy's voice sounded flat.

'Who's gone?'

'Me mum; with one of her fancy men. Dirty old – he is too. Even offered me a quid if I'd please 'im.'

Molly almost dropped the teapot in horror at the idea.

186

Tracy saw her concern. 'Don't be darft. I wouldn't let the likes of 'im anywhere near me.'

'What are you going to do now? You can't be there alone with your father. At least your mother stopped him from beating you too much.'

'Yer, I know. I reckon he might want a bit o' fun 'an all if me mum ain't around to satisfy 'im.'

'Molly turned white at the prospect. 'Tracy, you are to stay here with us. You can sleep in the spare room tonight.'

'An' what 'appens when 'e finds out where I am? 'E'd be round 'ere like a light.'

'Well, we'll find someone else from St. Gabriel's to put you up, and we won't tell him where you are.'

' 'E'd only get me on the way to school.'

'Then we'll contact the local social worker.'

'What! And 'ave me put in one of them 'omes. No thank yer.' She stood up, grabbed her case and made for the door. Molly intercepted her.

'Wait a minute, Tracy. We won't take any action until Christopher comes home. We need to do the wisest thing; you can understand that.'

'I ain't goin' in no 'ome. I don't care what the ol' man does. I ain't goin' in no 'ome.'

'I've said you can stay here.'

' 'Ow long for, eh? A week or two? What 'appens then? Where does I go then, eh? Tell me that!'

Molly fought to hold back the tears. She placed the mug of hot tea on the table beside Tracy. With one sweeping gesture the girl sent the scalding liquid crashing to the floor. 'Well, b—— answer me, then.' At last, she broke down and began to sob heavily. Ignoring the mess on the floor, Molly went over to her and held the girl in her arms. Tracy clung to her as if she was the last hope of survival.

'I'm sorry, I'm sorry.'

'Don't worry,' answered Molly, just as Christopher entered the kitchen. He took a quick glance at the floor and then searched his wife's eyes for an explanation.

'Tracy's mother has left home.'

Christopher stood speechless. All his wife's honourable ambitions for him had now come to this: the house-proud woman leaving her floor steaming with hot tea while she held this unwanted, unhappy child to her breast with obvious love and compassion.

'She'll stay here tonight,' she announced with authority.

'What about her father?' Christopher asked. Molly felt like replying with some choice words about him. Instead she simply said, 'There is no alternative. Besides, I want Tracy to stay.'

At that the girl drew away and for once looked straight at Molly. 'You don't mean that.'

'I do, Tracy. I want you to stay here. I shall be very upset if you don't.'

'But 'ow long for?'

'Until all this has blown over,' put in Christopher.

'And then what? Back to 'ell.'

'We would have no right to keep you here against your parents' wishes.'

'They don't care about me. I don't wanner taste what you've got 'ere if I 'ave ter go back to that lot.'

'And she's not going into a home.' Molly quickly countered the thought that was probably in Christopher's mind.

'Too b—— right, I'm not,' insisted Tracy. 'I'll put up wiv me father rather than that.'

Christopher felt that he should not rush into any hasty promises that he might regret later. 'Look, Tracy dear. None of us knows what is going to happen. You can stay here for as long as you need to.'

A sudden thought seemed to cross the girl's mind. 'I didn't come 'ere for this, yer know. Really, I didn't. It's just that there was nowhere else to go, and I needed some 'elp. But I'll wash yer dishes and I'll scrub yer floor, Mrs., honest I'll scrub it all clean.'

'Tracy, you will not come here to work for us, but to be one of the family,' said Molly.

That evening they awaited the bang on the door from Tracy's father. Instead, nothing. 'Probably gone down the boozer and got sloshed,' conjectured Tracy.

The explanation for his non-appearance was on the front page of the morning paper, together with a small photograph of a rough-looking, unshaven man of about forty. The family resemblance, though, could be detected. The brief report said that Tracy's father had been charged with causing grievous bodily harm to his wife and her lover in the latter's flat on the other side of town. Both were in hospital suffering from multiple wounds inflicted by the accused with a poker.

Obviously, Tracy would have to be told. She read the report with an expressionless face. 'Well, that's 'im out of the way for a good bit.' Then she began to cry. 'What will they say now?'

'Who?' asked Molly.

'All the kids at school. What will they say when they know that I'm living 'ere an' all?'

'You needn't go to school today,' said Christopher.

'Oh, yes I am,' protested Tracy. 'I wouldn't give that stuck-up bunch the pleasure of thinkin' I couldn't face 'em. Not on yer life. I've got me pride too, yer know.'

As soon as Tracy had left the house, Christopher telephoned the school and agreed to see the headmaster that morning. It was arranged through the welfare department that Tracy would remain in their charge, at least until her mother could decide on what should happen to her.

She adapted to life in the rectory surprisingly well, although she soon displayed a streak of stubbornness that was the result, no doubt, of having to fend for herself in her own home. She flatly refused to visit her mother in hospital, despite all Christopher could do to persuade her. 'No, no, no,' she would say. 'Never! The old cow went off and left me. Now she can rot in her stinking 'ospital bed.'

Molly's sermons on forgiving one another went unheeded. A letter from her mother arrived some four weeks after Tracy's arrival at the rectory. This would have been torn up if Christopher hadn't rescued it in time. The treacly endearments it contained belied the true situation. 'The old bitch only wants me back to cook and look after 'er,' which was probably true and the Deans knew it.

Christopher decided that he would go himself to the hospital, a course he soon regretted. After thanking him for looking after her charming daughter, Tracy's mother began to make a number of outrageous suggestions as to Christopher's true motives. He hastily withdrew, realising what a tight grip Satan had on some people; they seemed to be corrupt through and through. The thought that Tracy had spent her life in the midst of such corruption made him shudder. At least she could now know the healing of an environment of Christian love.

But he was too eager to see progress in Tracy's life. It was bad enough having to put up with her language; it was even worse that she showed no interest whatsoever in the Lord. She maintained that Christopher only believed because he was paid to do so, and although she continued her weekly visit to St. Gabriel's on Sunday morning, she still appeared to take no part in the service.

One day, after about three months, Tracy failed to return to the rectory after school. Several hours later

Christopher was alarmed enough to inform the police. All that could be discovered was that she was last seen entering the railway station with a youth of about twenty. Christopher and Molly never saw or heard from her again. Presumably she became one of the many lost youngsters in the big city. What had befallen her there they could only imagine.

A sense of complete failure now filled their lives.

'Where did we go wrong?' asked Molly. 'We tried to love her and to accept her. We didn't force our beliefs on her. During those few months that she was with us, she had a better life than she had ever known. It doesn't seem to make sense!'

'Nobody can force a person to accept love, my dear,' was the only reply that made sense to Christopher. 'We must simply go on loving.'

'Even when it doesn't produce results?'

'Even when it doesn't appear to produce results.'

'Oh, come on, Christopher! We've failed, and failed miserably.'

'Yes, but we have learned a great deal.'

'You mean, we have suffered from Tracy's moods and difficulties, all to no avail!'

'Do you regret having her here to live?'

'No, of course not!'

'Then you can expect that God has more to teach us in all this.'

'What, for instance?'

To that question Christopher had no answer. He only knew that if the love of Jesus was to be manifested at St. Gabriel's, there would be many more Tracys.

17

THERE HAD BEEN a variety of reactions in the church concerning Tracy. Some had frankly admired Christopher and Molly; others thought them foolish, while a few openly criticised them, feeling threatened by the dangers of facing too realistically the Lord's command to love. When Tracy disappeared, there were, accordingly, different feelings. Some shared in the Deans' sorrow and perplexity, others sighed with relief, and a few nodded their heads knowingly and were quick with their 'I told you so's'.

'I tell you one thing it has taught me, though, and that is the enormous influence environment has on the personality.' Christopher was talking to Paul in his study. 'Living in the same house as Tracy and listening to the lurid descriptions of her home life was a real eye-opener.'

'Isn't it amazing how many people have dark corners in their lives?' mused Paul. 'I'm not sure that I've met such a clear-cut case as Tracy, but even apparently "clean" people often have hatred, jealousy or a sense of failure which warps their thinking completely.'

'But isn't it great to see these things brought to God and destroyed with the power of His love? Sometimes I feel I'm doing more harm than good, dragging up people's past, but provided they have the right attitude to it, this confession can be the turning-point for many.'

'Like the two men from that firm in Waterloo Road, who left their jobs because of shady goings-on there,' said Paul. 'As soon as they had discussed the matter together they realised its importance, and actually taking the step of leaving was the beginning of a new depth of spiritual life for them.'

'And have you heard that Bob asked the other one to move in with his family? I'm beginning to lose count of the families that have extended themselves in some way. You started it all off, Paul, by suggesting to Claude that you would be better off together. Miss Trace looks ten years younger now that she has people to cook for and no more rent to worry about. In some cases it's worked out so well I don't know why we didn't think of it much earlier.'

'It's not so easy as that, though, Christopher. Imagine marrying for the first time at sixty, with all the habits you've acquired by then. That's what Claude is going through at the moment, and he's finding it difficult, I can tell you. One of the reasons I've come out tonight is that he loves having the record player on loud, especially when I want to read.'

Christopher smiled. 'It may not be much consolation to you, Paul, but the fact that your house is now known to be open to all and sundry for coffee, company and comfort has taken a great load from my back. I approve of this increased lay ministry idea. You wouldn't like to take over some of these filing cabinets as well, by any chance?'

For some time, Tom had felt that he was no longer at home in the business world and that God was calling him into a full-time ministry What was strange was that at first he felt no inclination towards ordination. He was obviously being greatly used by God in the counselling that he did on three evenings a week.

'Tom, I believe you already have your ministry,' Christopher said one day.

'Yes, but the pace is beginning to tell. I'm at work all day, counselling in the evenings, attending the study sessions, and hardly have any time to be with the family. That can't be right.'

'So what has to go?' asked Christopher.

'The study sessions can't go. I shall have nothing to give unless I am being fed myself. I could cut down on the counselling, but that doesn't seem to be right. It's the job that's out of place. But I can't just leave with no income to support the family.'

'Then we need to supply the income,'' suggested Christopher.

'Who do you mean by "we"?'

'St. Gabriel's, of course.'

'But I haven't received any formal training.'

'By man—or by God? The Holy Spirit has had you in hand for nearly two years now. And you are a greater instrument of His grace than many ordained clergymen that I know!'

'How will the rest of the church family view the idea?'

'I think with relief. Frankly, I'm fed up with everyone telling me how tired I'm looking, and that I need to rest more.'

'They're right, of course!'

'Don't you start. It's not words I need but someone available full-time to help.'

'Won't most people expect you to ask for a curate?'

'That would be the conventional thing to do. However, there's a shortage of clergy at present—and I really believe that God wants to develop this concept of lay ministry within the local church. It's time we were freed from the idea that anyone with a valid full-time ministry needs to have his collar round the wrong way!'

'Let's pray about it,' suggested Tom, 'and I'll talk to Ann. It would involve so many changes for us.'

Fortunately, the people of St. Gabriel's had by now grasped the fact that the Holy Spirit led God's people into ways of continual change. It was readily agreed at the parish meeting that Tom should be regarded as having a full-time pastoral ministry. Many had already benefited personally from his help and appreciated the need for him to be available to counsel those seeking God and His healing in their lives.

Tom and Ann received great encouragement as they began to grow accustomed to their new way of life. Several in the church believed that God was asking them to guarantee differing sums of money that would be used to support the Billings family. For Tom and Ann, there was the difficulty of accepting the Lord's generosity through their new-found friends.

One job Tom soon had was to lead small teams of lay people from the church who went to spend a week-end with other churches, sharing with them the vision of what God desired to do in the lives of his children. Such visits were always rewarding for those who were sent from St. Gabriel's, as well as for those who received these teams.

In spite of these week-ends it could hardly be said that there was a wild evangelistic fervour at St. Gabriel's— rather, a quiet persistence in prayer for the renewal of the whole Church and the acceptance of the opportunities provided to witness to the truth that had become so vividly real to them.

When Tom was at home for the week-end he was struck

by the change in the worship at St. Gabriel's. It was no longer a formality, but alive and vital, although the form of the service remained unaltered during this time. It was the hearts of the worshippers that had been changed. There was now a real sense of abiding together in the love and joy of the Lord. Even the children were beginning to enjoy worship!

'Christopher, we need another act of worship on Sundays.' Tom was speaking after one of the now daily prayer meetings. 'There doesn't seem to be time enough on a Sunday morning for God to do all that He wants to do. And I believe we need to have more opportunities to express freely this praise that God has put into our hearts, to allow the prayer gifts of the Spirit to be manifested and to give opportunity for a longer exposition of the Word.'

'People can receive that at the study session mid-week, Tom.'

'Our people can. What about the visitors? Once they have been to our teaching course, there is nothing else for them.'

'They are supposed to receive further teaching in the churches they come from.'

'But they don't. You know they don't.'

Christopher looked thoughtful. He had been careful to assure the clergy in surrounding churches that he was not interested in 'sheep-stealing'. Yet the truth of what Tom was saying couldn't be denied. Many were not receiving the teaching they needed, nor did they have sufficient opportunities for genuine fellowship. It was one thing to bring people into a new dimension of life in the Spirit, quite another to give them the sustenance they required to grow in that life.

'I don't know, Tom. The attendance at Sunday evening

services is in decline almost everywhere. Many places have stopped having them altogether.'

'That's an excuse, Christopher, and you know it. If we were to have an open service of praise here you wouldn't be able to stop people coming.'

'That is precisely what I'm afraid of, Tom. Some would be tempted to come here instead of where they belonged, and it would also be an attraction to those who don't mind going to services that are alive and meaningful, but who want to shirk what it means to be a responsible part of the Body of Christ.'

'We had better pray about it,' suggested Tom. 'I see your arguments, but the decision needs to be made in heaven, not through our reasoning.' The two men looked at one another and laughed.

'I wonder how many committee meetings that would have taken before?' said Christopher.

The whole church was faced with the problem and asked to pray. As far as the people of St. Gabriel's were concerned, such an opportunity for free worship was now needed, and it did not seem right to stifle that need because others might be attracted by a service of praise. It was decided, therefore, to hold such a service on Sunday evenings for an experimental period of three months.

The response was immediate. The size of the evening congregation doubled and continued to grow steadily. The first attempts at 'open' worship seemed very stilted. They needed to grow in confidence before more people would feel free to lead in prayer or to speak about the way God was working in their lives.

Many from other places came to receive the teaching that Christopher gave at these services. He found that people were willing to sit and listen for forty-five minutes or more, so great was their hunger for the Word of God. He made it abundantly clear that the visitors were welcome to come occasionally for teaching and fellowship, only so that they would be better equipped to commit themselves to God in the church where they already belonged.

As the months passed, so the freedom became more obvious and they began to experience a more faithful reflection of New Testament worship. What impressed Christopher most was that, although he planned nothing for each service, the Spirit of God led the service in a positive direction on every occasion. At the end, there would be the definite impression that God had been in charge; He had spoken and He had acted in the lives of His people. Usually there was a great sense of coming before the very throne of God.

Dear Mr. Dean,

I had never experienced worship before, not true worship. I wanted to give myself wholeheartedly to the Lord. Perhaps it would be true to say that I had never experienced God before, not in the way I did at St. Gabriel's on Sunday evening. I have always been afraid of experience; I was taught that it was pure emotionalism. I now realise how wrong that is. There was no attempt on your part to encourage emotionalism; people's hearts were simply flooded with God's love. And the singing! Oh, my word, it was beautiful, especially when everybody sang in the Spirit. I have never heard such a magnificent sound.

What I am writing to tell you is that something wonderful happened to me. For the first time in my life, I was enjoying God, the thrill of His presence. I only desired to give myself to Him in praise, when I felt a strange warmth in my left knee. I started to move my leg about, bending and flexing it. I am glad that others around me had their eyes closed, otherwise they must have thought me mad to be doing exercises in the middle of a service! I found that I could move my knee joint fully, without any pain. You may think that there is nothing unusual in that, but since having a serious accident when I was eleven, I have had only restricted movement (despite four operations!) and have suffered pain whenever any undue strain has been put on that leg.

It seems that God has healed me, and I didn't even ask Him to! All I wanted to do was to thank Him for His wonderful love, and to tell everyone what He had just done for me. But I didn't dare; I am such a coward. Please forgive me. I felt I had to write and tell you, so that you can rejoice with me. In your own words (last Sunday) 'Praise our wonderful Lord.'

May He continue to bless your ministry,

Amanda Corey

Christopher wrote a brief reply and placed the letter in a rapidly thickening file containing others of a similar nature. He decided to write on the front cover 'To God be the glory, great things He has done.'

Certainly, these testimonies were a further confirmation that they had been right to begin this open service of praise; God was obviously using it in many important ways. Christopher secretly longed for the time when they would not need to welcome so many visitors from other churches, because they could find the same praise, the same love and power within the churches to which they already belonged. He could, however, thank God that the warmth of this love was reaching the hearts of so many.

Thelma Blainey was one of the few exceptions.

'It's no good, Vicar. I have been part of St. Gabriel's since I was a small girl and we have never had to put up with all these people. It's always been nice and friendly before. Not too many of us—and we've known one another for years. If this persists I shall have to go elsewhere to worship. I only want to be quiet and to keep myself to myself. You understand?'

Christopher understood. His heart went out to the few 'Thelmas'. How so many important things could go on around them without their apparently being moved at all spiritually, he could not grasp. What was clear was that Thelma preferred a few to worship God, rather than many; she wanted people to be 'friendly' rather than committed to one another in love, and the church was to consist of her contemporaries and not those 'new' people! He would have to suffer the sadness that Jesus must have experienced when some of His disciples left Him, because His teaching was too hard for them. Unhappily, not all those who opposed the purpose of God ended like Claude Winter, a stout witness of the living Christ.

'You cannot alter the commands of God,' reflected Christopher, 'and if you love Him, you don't want to!'

18

'IF ONLY WE could accept what we wanted and leave the rest,' Paul Rivers said.

'Especially the parts we don't understand,' added Claude Winter.

'That's the problem with the Bible. There was a time when we understood little and believed little of what is written in the Word. Now that the Holy Spirit is bringing things to life, you realise that you cannot sidestep many of the issues that you have been avoiding for years, or have never been aware of. Neither can you rationalise them away.'

'I can well remember the struggle I had with my intellect. "You're using it like a filter," Christopher told me, "accepting only what you want or can understand. God is greater than your mind or your intellect. You need to submit, Claude," he said, "submit your intellect to God. Let Him be Lord of your thinking, otherwise you will reduce Him to the size of your limited understanding." It was a struggle; I don't mind admitting it, either.'

Paul smiled. He remembered the time when Claude would have prided himself on his intellect. 'The trouble is,' he continued, 'it seems that many want to misrepresent you by saying that you are anti-intellectual. That's nonsense. Of course God has given us our ability to think, but He doesn't want us to misuse that gift by attempting to shrink Him to our size, to reduce Him from almightiness and perfection or to believe that His demands for us are less than they really are.'

'All right, all right,' said Paul. 'You don't have to convince me. I'm on His side—remember?' Claude laughed.

His stroke had left him with a pronounced limp, a constant reminder of his months of rebellion, but, as far as Claude was concerned, a healthy reminder. He and Paul were walking home after one of the most crucial meetings they had ever attended at the rectory, during the years of renewal at St. Gabriel's. They were faced with the question: What did it mean to lay down their lives for their friends?

'You know,' said Paul, avoiding a late-night dog-walker, 'it's been clear to me for some time that your moving in was only the first step in the giving over of my house to God's purposes. We've needed this time to settle down ourselves, but now we should think further afield. There are so many people who need the security of a Christian household, if only temporarily. How can we counsel and pray with people and then send them back to the very situation that is aggravating or even causing their problem?'

'I agree,' said Claude, 'in theory. But what about Christopher's latest proposition?'

That night Christopher had introduced the two men to David and Sarah Miles, a young married couple whom neither had met before. Sarah was seven months pregnant.

'David and Sarah are moving into the district,' explained Christopher. 'David is to teach history at the comprehensive school and Sarah is finishing work for obvious reasons. They need somewhere to live.'

Claude looked at Paul. The peace of their home was apparently to be shattered by the cries of a new-born infant. For Claude that would be a new experience, but Paul wondered whether he was not too old to go back to such things. 'What do you have in mind?' Paul asked Christopher.

'Not that David and Sarah should come and lodge with you I cannot see much purpose in that. I believe God has been leading this young couple in a particular way. David, perhaps you had better explain yourself.'

The young man hesitated as if deciding where he should begin. 'We have been married for eighteen months. Both of us have been Christians for about five years. When we decided to become engaged we gave our life together to the Lord and asked Him to use us in whatever way He wanted. We didn't want to have a selfish marriage, building up a place of our own, surrounded by our own possessions. Financially that wasn't possible, anyway; I was a student and Sarah wasn't exactly earning a fortune. We had a small semi-furnished flat and managed reasonably well. But we knew that God had some plan for us. About a month ago, I was given the history job which would mean moving into this district.'

Sarah was bursting to tell the men the next part of their story. 'I was at home while David went for the interview and while I was praying it was as if the Lord was saying, "St. Gabriel's", or rather, "Go to St. Gabriel's." I couldn't understand that. I knew Gabriel was an archangel so I looked up the scripture references about him but none of them seemed relevant.'

David again took up the narrative. 'Sarah was delighted about the job but I couldn't understand this St. Gabriel's business either. We'd never heard of your church, you see, coming from so far away. Anyhow, we started to pray about a place to live and this time it was my turn. "You are to live at St. Gabriel's." We were still perplexed. "Perhaps St. Gabriel's is a place," we thought. So we took out the atlas and looked for a village or town around here with that name.'

'And found none,' said Paul. 'So what next?'

'I was resting one afternoon,' answered Sarah, 'when I had a flash of inspiration. I couldn't wait for David to come home.'

'And when I did she didn't waste any time telling me,' said David with a smile. 'You see, we have wanted to live in a Christian community, like you read about at the end of the second chapter of Acts. We'd never been attracted by any of the communes we'd heard about and were content that God would lead us into a community if that was where He wanted us. Sarah's flash of inspiration, as she calls it, was that we were to live in community at St. Gabriel's. "Fine," I said, "if only we can find where it is." '

' "Let's go and look then," I suggested. David was rather reluctant, what with me being pregnant and the cost of fares these days, but eventually he agreed.'

'I must say that I felt rather foolish,' admitted David. 'We arrived at the station without the slightest idea where to go. So I sent one of those prayer darts up to heaven. "Where to now, Lord?" The extraordinary thing was that He answered. Not that I heard anything. Sarah tugged at my arm. "This way," she said. For the next ten minutes we walked, and all the time she seemed convinced that she knew the way, although we must have made several turnings in that time.'

'I did know the way,' protested Sarah. 'I'm not sure how; I just knew.'

'Well, we stopped outside your house, Mr. Rivers. "That's St. Gabriel's," Sarah said. There was no nameplate on the gate. I thought that the pregnancy was making her a little funny and I was most reluctant when she suggested that I knock on the door. Eventually, I agreed and was tremendously relieved when there was no reply.' Claude and Paul both smiled. 'But her ladyship here was not to be deterred. "We'll go next door and ask," she said. So we did just that. A little old lady came to the door. "No, that is not St. Gabriel's," she said; "that is where Mr. Rivers lives. I don't think he has given the house a name." Poor Sarah! She looked so desperately disappointed that I asked the old lady is she knew of a house called by that name, more out of hope than anything. "No, my boy," she said.' They grinned at David's imitation of Miss Barclay. ' "The only St. Gabriel's I know is the church round the corner!" '

'You can imagine how surprised we were,' continued Sarah. ' "How can we live in a church?" I asked. The poor old lady didn't reply to that. She politely excused herself and shut the door.'

The men could contain themselves no longer and burst into laughter. 'Poor old Miss Barclay,' said Claude. 'I'm sorry. What did you do?'

'We went round to the church,' said David, 'just to have a look for some clue as to what this was all about. We picked up a copy of this month's magazine and saw the rector's article on the need for community households. We were staggered. So we came round to the rectory.'

'Quite a story, isn't it?' suggested Christopher.

'I'm not sure that I understand the part about my house,' said Paul with some caution in his voice.

'Oh, that's the community house,' said Sarah lightly.

'Is it indeed?' answered Paul, raising his eyebrows.

'Oh, I'm sorry,' countered Sarah quickly, thinking that she had upset him. 'I mean that is how it seemed to me. I may be wrong, of course.'

'No, my dear. I don't think you're wrong,' said Paul. 'God has been leading us in that direction for some time.

To be honest, I didn't expect things to develop quite so soon—or in this way. You've given us a great deal to think and pray about.'

'David and Sarah are staying overnight with us,' said Christopher. 'I thought it would be good for them to join in our worship tomorrow and we can also get to know them a little better.' He turned to the young couple. 'Now, if you don't mind, I'd like to talk to Paul and Claude alone for a while.'

'Of course; we understand,' said David. They stood up, shook hands with Paul and Claude and left the study.

'I'm sorry to land this on you in such a way,' said Christopher. 'I thought it best that you saw them for yourselves.'

'They seem a pleasant young couple,' answered Claude.

'They do,' agreed Paul. 'However, you have always maintained that there should be some purpose in a household. What purpose would be served by them coming to live with us?'

'First, I think we need to know if God is really in all this,' answered Christopher, 'then we can trust Him to show us His purpose. They are not idle loafers, but two hard-working young people who love the Lord. The way He has led them seems incredible. They certainly knew nothing about St. Gabriel's when they arrived here. In fact, my talk with them was a revelation for them both.'

The two men left the rectory with very mixed feelings. If God was in all this, their quiet orderly lives were about to be disrupted.

At the end of the morning service Paul turned to Claude. 'We ought to invite them to lunch.'

'Had exactly the same idea myself,' admitted Claude.

The young couple accepted the invitation. They were overawed at the size of the house, although with five bedrooms and two rooms in the attic, it was hardly a mansion. Sarah insisted on doing the cooking, and demonstrated her considerable skill in that department. For her it was a luxury to work in a well-equipped kitchen.

The highlight of their visit was not the lunch, however, but the sense of unity they enjoyed when they prayed together afterwards. The Lord's presence seemed to confirm that He had some purpose in bringing their lives together.

'I am a cautious man,' said Paul before their departure. 'I feel it right for us to offer you a home when you first move here. However, we will allow God to lead us concerning what our commitment should be to one another. This may only be a temporary arrangement; it may develop into something more permanent. Will you come on that understanding?'

'Paul, we've had the most extraordinary week-end of our lives. I think that we are both concerned that our standard of living may be somewhat different from yours, and we would want to pay our own way. That may be difficult.'

'Perhaps it's our standard of living that needs looking at in that case,' commented Claude. 'I didn't think we were extravagant, but then our student days are further behind us than yours!'

'I'm sure that the details will be worked out easily enough if we are in the Lord's will,' said Paul as they departed.

At first, those words seemed prophetic. David was more nervous than Sarah in their new surroundings, yet he proved to be a tremendous help in the work of the church. He had a flair for relating to teenagers and soon joined the leadership group of the rapidly-expanding youth fellowship. His guitar playing was also much appreciated at the various prayer meetings and he seemed to have the ability to direct people to the Lord in praise. Sarah quickly established contact with some of the young mothers in the church, and Paul and Claude had to grow accustomed to arriving home to the sight of two or three prams on the doorstep.

When Sarah was confined to her room for the delivery of Timothy, the older men were convinced that they missed her presence around the house as much as her husband did. They were certainly pleased to dance attendance upon her, even to the extent of placing the numerous nappies in soak when asked to do so.

But problems there were. Each of the men realised very quickly that their independence was further threatened, that they were committed to this young couple and were no longer free to make arbitrary decisions about the running of their affairs without reference to them.

'At least you can read in peace tonight, Paul. I can't have the record player on with all those guitars strumming away in there.' Claude was good-humouredly making mugs of coffee for the four teenagers who had just arrived to see David.

'I could, but Sarah has lent the book I'm reading to one of her friends this afternoon, thinking I had finished it. She must have a constant stream of people here from the number of books she hands out.'

'We don't do too badly in the evening for visitors either. It's like living on Paddington station sometimes.'

The doorbell rang. Paul laughed and moved into the hall.

'Oh for the good old days when I didn't see anybody between leaving work at five-thirty and nine the next morning!'

19

CHRISTOPHER LOOKED HARD at the words before him. 'You did not choose me, but I chose you.' He remembered the first visits from Alan. Yes, it was true that God had sought him out and found him. He had never aspired to the type of ministry that God had chosen for him. It had been an exhausting few years, yet they had proved to be infinitely rewarding, seeing God do so many important things in the lives of His people.

Occasionally he was genuinely perplexed to know how it had become so easy for the churches to fail completely to be the Body of Christ. To think that he had once been one of the stoutest defenders of the ecclesiastical machinery! Not that he advocated doing away with the structure of the Church. All that had happened at St. Gabriel's had snown that it was possible to find new life and the freedom to express that life within the existing structures. They might need renewing, but not destroying.

Molly disturbed his thoughts when she entered the study with a cup of tea.

'I'm sorry. Were you praying?'

'No, my dear, only thinking.'

'What about?'

'Being chosen by God . . . His Church . . . renewal.'

'Four years ago such things would not have entered your mind.' She placed an arm affectionately on his shoulder. 'Or mine.'

'The Lord has done many wonderful things, Molly. There is so much to be grateful for. And yet there are still so many things that need to happen here.'

'What, more?' said Molly with protest in her voice. 'I should have thought there was enough going on already.'

'Yes, yes there is. We don't want another spate of over-activity. Yet there are so many things to sort out: the new structure of leadership, relationships, faith, especially in regard to healing and guidance. We have a whole new set of problems. But I grant you that they are ones that I would much rather have than the old ones.'

'Especially the ones with your wife!'

'I didn't say that!'

'No, I did. Why God chose me to be your wife, I shall never understand. I could never be part of your ministry.'

'How many times have I told you . . .'

'I know, I know. The Lord wants me to be your wife, not your assistant. Don't worry, my days of trying to manipulate you or your ministry are definitely over. In any case, I should never be able to out-manoeuvre the Holy Spirit.'

'Look at this,' Christopher said, handing her a letter that lay open on his desk. It was an invitation from the Bishop to give the address at the Diocesan Festival to be held in the cathedral in three months' time.

'Are you going to accept?' she asked.

'Yes, of course. It shows a considerable measure of confidence in all that is happening here.'

'My dear man, you would hardly expect him to be unhappy. The fruit speaks for itself.'

'There are those who object and they would be quick to

tell the Bishop so. But he is a man of God and he appreci-
ates that the ways of the Spirit cannot be compacted into
any man-made schemes.'

They were interrupted by the doorbell. Molly returned
to the study.

'Lucy Cartwright is here again, dear. What do I do?'

Christopher sighed. Lucy had been a problem for some
time, so much so that Christopher had spent time in prayer
that morning asking God what he should do about her. His
eyes had been opened to several truths, not only about
Lucy, but also about himself. This was an interview he had
been dreading, for he knew that it could be very unpleasant
for both of them.

'You had better show her in.' He stood up. 'Hello, Lucy.
Come and sit down.'

'I don't think you wanted to see me,' she began.

'Why should you imagine that?'

'Because I'm a nuisance to you. I know I am. I'm a
nuisance to everyone.'

'Why do you think that?' asked Christopher.

'See! You don't deny it, do you?'

'Lucy, this is the fourth time this week that you have
been to see me.'

'It's your job, isn't it?'

'In a way. There are many others to see as well as you,
and they usually make appointments.'

'Oh well, I'll go then.' She made as if to leave.

'All right then, Lucy. Goodbye.' She stood in the middle
of the room, stunned. This was the crucial moment and
Christopher knew it. Before, he would have tried to assure
her that he did want to talk to her at any time that she felt
the need. He would have told her to sit down and would
have tried to placate her. And all the time he would have
imagined that this was the loving thing to do. That morn-

ing, his eyes had been opened to see the ways in which Lucy was manipulating him through her own insecurity. At heart, Christopher was still very soft, and that meant that at times he was unloving. It would be much better, he realised, to be firm and not allow Lucy to manipulate him any longer. That was going to be tough for him as well as for her.

'You don't really love me, then. After all this talk about loving one another that I hear at St. Gabriel's! You don't love me; you want me to go.'

'It was you who suggested leaving,' pointed out Christopher.

'Don't play with words,' said Lucy angrily. 'The plain truth is that you are a hypocrite. You say you love me but you don't.'

'Then why have I spent so much time with you recently, talking about your problems?' he asked.

'Just for appearances' sake.'

'Before whom was I appearing?'

'Don't be sarcastic. You're always the same. You have to be in the right. I'll go and tell them all what you're really like. You don't know the meaning of the word "love".'

Christopher swallowed hard. This was proving more difficult than he had anticipated. He remained calm. 'I've told you that you are free to go if you wish.'

'I won't come back.'

'That is up to you.'

'Is this how you treat your flock? You're supposed to go and seek the one who is lost, and all you want to do is to get rid of me.'

'Lucy, I've had enough of your self-pity, your threats, your spiritual blackmail and your sheer manipulation. If you want to go, then go. If you have something more to say then sit down and say it.' At first he thought he had gone too far. She turned and walked to the door, then stopped. She stared at him. He returned the stare, knowing that it was important for him not to flinch beneath the accusing glare.

Lucy was the first to lower her eyes. Almost sheepishly, she returned to her chair and sat down. Christopher waited for a moment and then continued with what he knew had to be said. 'Lucy, you have had many difficulties in your life and I have tried to share them with you in these last weeks. However, you have traded on this with your self-pity. I have been prepared to ask God to heal you, but I don't believe you have really wanted that healing. You have spent most of your life trying to encourage people to feel sorry for you. I don't altogether blame you for that, because of the nature of your problems. But this pattern of behaviour must stop, otherwise you will never be capable of an enriching relationship, either with God or with people. If others don't pity you, then you bully and pressurise them into feeling that they ought to—like accusing me of being unloving. Or you threaten me. It must all finish, Lucy. You can see that, can't you?'

'How?' she asked quietly. She didn't argue or disagree with him.

'God will give you the grace, if you truly want to be healed. Do you?'

'I don't know.' Her head was still bowed. Slowly, she looked up at him. 'I could hate you.'

Christopher could see the anger in her eyes. 'Why? Because I have made you face the truth?'

'I suppose so.' They lapsed into silence. 'Will you help me?' Lucy asked after a while.

'If you want help, rather than pity, I will certainly do anything I can.' Lucy went to the door. 'Thank you,' she said and left.

'That seemed rather inconclusive,' said Molly, when Christopher had finished his account of the interview.

'In one way, I agree. This is going to be a long job. There are many years of manipulation behind that girl and she is not going to be able to change her pattern of behaviour overnight. But you know, Molly, I'm still too soft. I very nearly gave in to her.'

'But, Christopher, you have stood up to people in the past. Remember what happened ages ago when there was all that trouble with Claude.'

'Ah, but this is more subtle, dear, much more subtle. Claude was obviously wrong in the things he said. Lucy appeared to be right. She made me feel condemned, so that I was prepared to see her when she wanted me to, and to do everything possible to keep her happy. Only yesterday Paul said to me, "That poor girl Lucy, she does have some problems." And she has been taking some of Tom's time as well. We need to watch for those who delight in sharing their problems with everyone. What's for supper? I'm hungry.'

'There is a great sense of being among the elect of God.' Christopher's visitor eased himself back in the chair. It had been a good lunch. In fact, it had been a good week, much to his surprise. The Reverend Maurice Drury had come to spend a few days at St. Gabriel's to see what was happening there. His interest had been aroused from reports he had heard, but he came with suspicion and doubt, wanting to find fault so that he could dismiss the matter from his mind. What he found was so different from what he had anticipated! Instead of setting himself up as judge,

214

he had found himself humbled by the sincerity of the people of St. Gabriel's, by their simple love for God and their commitment to one another. Never before had he experienced such joy and praise in worship, or people opening their lives and their homes to one another and to those in need in quite this way. And all this within the context of an ordinary parish church!

Perhaps the most important thing was what had happened to him personally during his visit. He had discovered a new sense of vocation, of being chosen by God. Together with Christopher, he had laid his life and ministry before Him and prayed that he would be filled with the Holy Spirit and empowered to fulfil the purpose that God had for him. Since that prayer, Maurice had entered into a new dimension of joy. He had laid hands on a woman crippled with arthritis and seen her locked joints freed by God's power. He had experienced the great joy of leading a young woman into a living relationship with the Lord at the end of a Sunday evening service when she had asked for help. And he had made friendships that he reckoned would be long-lasting. Yes, he was a son of God; he knew himself to be this, and he could look forward to a new kind of ministry in the future.

Maurice was one of a series of ministers from every conceivable denomination who found their way to St. Gabriel's, seeking new purpose and power in their ministries.

'It is a matter of realising that God has chosen us,' Maurice continued, 'of knowing that we are sons of God, filled with the Spirit of God, who will bear fruit in our lives.'

'That is the promise,' agreed Christopher. He had heard many giving expression in similar ways to the new-found wonder of God in their lives.

'I can hardly wait to get back to my own church and begin this new ministry.'

'Well, remember to take things steadily,' advised Christopher. 'It took some time for things to develop here. You don't want to begin by frightening people with your new revelations. God tells us to seek His wisdom. Don't go rushing in and expect God to follow or to pick up the pieces when there is a crash. Follow the leading of His Spirit, wait upon Him, abide in Jesus.'

Maurice recognised the wisdom of the advice. 'The Spirit will have to restrain me as well as encourage me,' he quipped.

'Make sure you allow Him to do just that,' cautioned Christopher.

'This concept of loving one another is so important,' Maurice enthused.

'Don't expect people to commit themselves to one another until they have first committed their lives to God,' warned Christopher. 'You can't begin by rushing people into community. That would only cause harm. Begin where people are now—where you were when you came here. They need to know that they are chosen and accepted by God. They need to experience His forgiveness and the empowering of the Holy Spirit in their lives. And you will have to lead them one by one to that point. There are no short cuts, no instant successes. There is a great deal of hard work and heartache before you if you want to see your church renewed.'

'It'll be worth it, though. That's what I've seen here. No matter what it costs, it'll be worth it.'

'It is God-given, Maurice. It is His work and it is for His glory. We are a very imperfect bunch, you know. God still has a great deal to work out among us.'

'You finish one meal, you digest it and you are ready for

216

another,' said Molly thoughtfully. Christopher smiled at
the simplicity of what she said.

'Long may the hunger for more of God continue,' he
said. 'You, Maurice, have first to stimulate that hunger in
others.'

'I only hope we can become another St. Gabriel's.'

'No, don't ever wish that. Let God do that work in your
church which is His unique plan for your situation. Here
you have been given a vision of what kind of things He can
do when He is allowed scope in people's lives. Don't try to
confine your congregation within a St. Gabriel's mould.'

Once again, Maurice knew he had heard important
advice.

'I feel more people should get to hear what you have
learnt here. Have you considered preaching tours, writing
a book...'

'If God wants anything like that, He will have to create
a new metric day with one hundred hours in it!'

20

THE CATHEDRAL WAS filled to capacity for the Festival. In
the transepts sat the clergy in their robes, while the lofty
proportions of the nave absorbed upwards of two thousand
people from all over the diocese. The choir had entered in
procession and demonstrated their musical ability. Now

the sound of the organ filled the whole building, almost drowning the host of voices which it accompanied.

For weeks this occasion had been in the back of Christopher's mind. He sensed its importance, yet he had been unable to determine what it was that God desired to speak through him. In vain he seemed to wait upon the Lord for His Word for this moment. At the same time, he received assurance and peace that God would use this time for His glory.

Christopher prayed quietly in tongues amidst the noise of the singing and the organ. Still there seemed to be an emptiness, nothing to say. It was time to move to the pulpit. As he mounted the steps he was surprised at his calmness—no fear, no panic. This, after all, was like any other occasion. 'Open your mouth wide and I will fill it.' God had not failed him before, and He was not likely to fail him now.

He looked out over the sea of heads, mostly buried in the service sheets. The strange feeling of compassion that came upon him was a sign of the love which God had put into his heart. Surely the Lord looked upon these people at this moment and desired to speak His love to them?

The echo of the music died away. Christopher's voice sounded hollow and metallic as the amplification system reproduced the words of his prayer: 'Gracious Father, speak to us your children and give us hearts that hear and receive your word . . .' Clothing rustled, chairs screeched, as the great congregation sat down, ready to listen. There was silence. Christopher had no words to fill it, either. The faces of the people were turned upwards towards him in anticipation. Not that he was conscious of them. He could not see through the haze of tears that rolled down his cheeks.

He knew that God had put a new power and authority

into his preaching in recent years. Perhaps he had been looking to Him to manifest that authority on this occasion. Instead, the Lord gave him only tears.

The tension increased: not an embarrassed silence, an expectant one. Only the Dean of the cathedral looked with some consternation towards the pulpit, wondering whether he would need to come to Christopher's assistance in some way.

Christopher made no attempt to wipe the tears from his cheeks. He could only hear the faint sound caused by them falling onto the reading-desk in front of him.

When he finally spoke, his voice was almost a whisper. 'I weep because my Father weeps. I stand in this lofty pulpit and I see a vast throng of God's people, and instead of words to say, He gives me tears to weep. Are they my tears, or His? Does God sit on His lofty throne and look upon His Church and weep? Or does He rejoice in what He sees?

'He looks upon His Son and He rejoices, for His Son accomplished what He was sent to do. He lived the life of love, of obedience, even to the point of death. The Father is pleased with the sacrifice which He offers—it is holy and acceptable to Him.

'And God looks upon those who, by His gracious act, He has placed in His Son. What He has done for them is good, very good.

'Yet, He is sad; He weeps. For He looks upon His Church and He searches for His Son. He strains to see the love, the power, the joy, the life, the peace that He gives. "These are now my sons," He says, "and where is the life of my Son? Must my Spirit remain locked within them for ever? Will they not turn to me with their whole hearts? Will they not seek my ways? Will they not hear my voice? Must I come among them with justice and wrath, with judgment and righteous anger? Must I prove to them that I am holy, that I am God, before they will honour me with their hearts as well as with their lips? Where is my Son?"

'And God listens. He hears the protests of the theologians, He sees the anguish of the afflicted; still He beholds the self-righteousness of the Pharisees and the legalism of the lawyers. And He asks, "Where is my Son?" He sees the mounting piles of administration, the concern for prestige and position and honour. He chooses not to look upon the secret sins that are committed behind locked doors, for shame and dishonour do not befit Him. Instead He looks with hope for His Son.

'He peers into the hearts of His beloved ones. He sifts their motives and intentions, and He rejoices over every occasion when He can bestow blessing, when He can give His love and heal the sick and raise the dead. He rejoices, for then He sees Jesus. And He is glad, for others see His Son too.

'He listens to the sounds of praise that ascend from every part of the earth. His ear sifts the pure from the discordant. He is pleased when the worship comes from those made one by the power of His Spirit, for then He hears Jesus. That blesses Him and makes Him glad.

'And God looks out upon His world and His sadness is mixed with anger. For He has sent His son, He has proclaimed His Word, He has made atonement for the sins of men. Yet in their folly, men still abuse God and deny Him. They do not heed His ways, neither do they care for Him. There is no gratitude in their hearts for His love, no desire for submission to Him or obedience to His will.

'So God looks again upon His Church and He demands, "Where is my Son? Have I not given Him to you? Have I not poured out my Spirit upon you? Have I not made you the sons of God? Are you not parts of the Body of my Son?

' "Where is He? What have you done with His love, His power, His truth? Where have you concealed Him? The world waits with groaning for my sons to be revealed."

' "Am I to pity you?" says the Lord. "Am I to look upon the life that you live as my Church and believe that I am honoured by it? Am I to come down from heaven and bow in worship before you and say, 'I have come to do your will, my people?' " '

Christopher paused. His voice had increased in volume as he had been speaking. Once again he almost whispered as he continued.

' "My dear beloved children, hear my Word to you to-day. For it is my desire to restore you. You are the house-hold of God, my chosen, my elect. I would make of you a mighty nation, a bride fit for my Son when He returns in triumph to claim His own.

' " You are the temple of my Spirit, the Body of my Son, and I shall renew you that men may know that you are my disciples. So return to me, my people. Give yourselves to me in repentence and I shall give to you the crown of life. No longer put your confidence in the ways of men; let your trust be in me alone."

' "Behold, I stand at the door and knock; if anyone hears my voice and opens the door, I will come in to him and eat with him, and he with me. He who conquers, I will grant him to sit with me on my throne, as I myself con-quered and sat down with my Father on His throne. He who has an ear, let him hear what the Spirit says to the churches." '

Colin Urquhart

ANYTHING YOU ASK

This book is strong meat. It will be talked
about, argued about, and can revolutionise
your life.

Jesus makes many astonishing promises of
the response that God's children can expect
to their prayers. But experience, for many
Christians, seems to fall far short. Why?

Here is the teaching of Jesus on prayer and
faith. Colin Urquhart shows, with examples
from his personal ministry, how people can
learn to pray with faith *and see God
answering their prayers.*

Colin Urquhart

IN CHRIST JESUS

'Wherever I travel I come across "defeated" Christians. Should they have to resign themselves to such defeat? Is it possible to know victory over temptation, weakness, futility and spiritual inadequacy?' asks Colin Urquhart.

In Christ Jesus offers, not new forms of healing or new prayer techniques, but a clear, thrilling statement of what God has done for mankind through Jesus. Some have been Christians for many years and although familiar with the Scriptures, have never learned how to live in the power of these truths, or to be set free by them.

Colin Urquhart here gives the heart of his teaching: how we can know Christ's power for ourselves.